T0063857

TOP **10**
RIO DE JANEIRO

Top 10 Rio de Janeiro Highlights

The Top 10 of Everything

Welcome to Rio de Janeiro............**5**

Exploring Rio de Janeiro **6**

Rio de Janeiro Highlights **10**

Corcovado.....................................**12**

Parque Nacional da Tijuca **14**

Sugar Loaf Mountain...................**16**

Mosteiro de São Bento **18**

Museu Nacional de
  Belas Artes **20**

Jardim Botânico...........................**24**

Museu Histórico Nacional...........**26**

Praça XV **28**

Praia de Copacabana...................**30**

Ipanema and Leblon
  Beachlife.....................................**32**

Moments in History **36**

Museums and Art Galleries........**38**

Beaches...**40**

Outdoor Activities **42**

Soccer..**44**

Off the Beaten Path **46**

Activities for Children **48**

Bars and Nightclubs....................**50**

Restaurants...................................**52**

Shopping.......................................**54**

Rio de Janeiro for Free................**56**

Carnaval Parades and Balls **58**

Festivals and Shows **60**

CONTENTS

Rio de Janeiro Area by Area

Centro **64**

The Guanabara Bay Beach
    Neighborhoods **70**

Lagoa, Gávea, and
    Jardim Botânico **76**

Santa Teresa and Lapa **82**

Copacabana, Ipanema,
    and Leblon **90**

Western Beaches **96**

Streetsmart

Getting Around **104**

Practical Information **106**

Places to Stay **112**

General Index **118**

Acknowledgments **124**

Phrase Book **126**

Selected Street Index **128**

Within each Top 10 list in this book, no hierarchy of quality or popularity is implied. All 10 are, in the editor's opinion, of roughly equal merit.

   Throughout this book, floors are referred to in accordance with American usage; i.e., the "first floor" is at ground level.

Title page, front cover, and spine *Aerial view of Rio de Janeiro's skyline, Praia Vermelha Beach, and Copacabana Beach in the distance*
Back cover, clockwise from top left *Tram running across Arcos da Lapa; Copacabana at dusk; cycling along Ipanema beach; Escadaria Selarón; the spectacular Cristo Redentor statue*

The rapid rate at which the world is changing is constantly keeping the DK Eyewitness team on our toes. While we've worked hard to ensure that this edition of Rio de Janeiro is accurate and up-to-date, we know that opening hours alter, standards shift, prices fluctuate, places close and new ones pop up in their stead. So, if you notice we've got something wrong or left something out, we want to hear about it. Please get in touch at **travelguides@dk.com**

Welcome to
Rio de Janeiro

With its postcard-perfect beaches, exciting foodie scene, and rhythmic *samba* beats, Rio offers a feast for the senses. This vibrant city is home to the biggest Carnaval in the world and the beautiful game of *futebol*, but perhaps what makes it truly special are its locals, or *Cariocas*, known for their irrepressible love of life. With *Eyewitness Top 10 Rio de Janeiro, it's yours to explore.*

We share *Cariocas*' passion for their beloved hometown and one of Brazil's best cities, with its natural wonders of **Pão de Açúcar**, and **Corcovado**, and the endless string of beaches from **Copacabana** to **Barra da Tijuca** and beyond. Then there's the year-round tropical heat, best enjoyed under a palm tree with a zesty *caipirinha* in hand. **Santa Teresa's** arty back streets, the verdant splendor of **Jardim Botânico**, and the wildlife-filled **Tijuca National Park** offer more beauty and relaxation.

Days are well spent here touring the city's well-preserved architectural sites, such as the **Mosteiro de São Bento**, or the wandering **Museu Nacional de Belas Artes**, home to one of Latin America's finest art collections. When evening beckons, Rio's entertainment scene is superb: there are spectacular *samba* shows, renowned *bossanova* and edgy *baile* funk clubs, and traditional *gafieira* dancehalls. The city's culinary scene doesn't disappoint either, offering everything from gourmet French cuisine and unique Amazonian delicacies to blowout Brazilian barbecues.

Whether you're coming for a weekend or a week, our Top 10 guide brings together the best of everything the city has to offer, from the coolest nightclubs to a year-round roster of festivals. The guide has useful tips throughout, from ideas on budget-friendly activities to how to avoid the crowds, plus eight easy-to-follow itineraries designed to tie together a clutch of sights in a short space of time. Add inspiring photography and detailed maps, and you've got the essential, pocket-sized travel companion. **Enjoy the book, and enjoy Rio de Janeiro**.

Clockwise from top: Cristo Redentor, Carnaval performers, the cable car on Sugar Loaf Mountain, café on Copacabana Beach, Escadaria Selarón, Museu de Arte Contemporânea

Exploring Rio de Janeiro

With its dazzling attractions and activities, Rio de Janeiro spoils visitors for choice. Whether you come for a few days or longer, you'll want to make the most of your time in this amazing city. Here are some ideas of how to spend two or four days' sightseeing in Rio de Janeiro.

Ipanema, one of Rio's big beaches, is overlooked by the Dois Irmãos mountain.

Two Days in Rio de Janeiro

Day ❶
MORNING

Take the funicular up to **Corcovado** (see pp12–13); return downtown to visit Rio's historic sights around **Praça XV** (see pp28–9), including **Mosteiro de São Bento** (see pp18–19).

AFTERNOON

Relax on the beach in **Copacabana** (see pp30–31). Stroll along the seafront Avenida Atlântica and have a drink at one of its street cafés.

Day ❷
MORNING

Go for a hike around **Parque Nacional da Tijuca** (see pp14–15)

before unwinding with a walk under the shady palm trees of the **Jardim Botânico** (see pp24–5).

AFTERNOON

Browse **Ipanema**'s (see pp32–3) trendy boutiques, then ride the cable car up **Sugar Loaf Mountain** (see pp16–17) to watch the sun set over the city. Visit Bohemian **Lapa** (see pp82–5) and go for a dance in a buzzing *samba* club.

Cosme Vel
stat

COSME
VELHO

FUNICULAR

Corcovado

Parque Nacional
da Tijuca

LAGOA

Jardim
Botânico

Lagoa
Rodrigo
de Freitas

Fundaçã
Eva Klab

Ipanema's
boutiques

IPANEMA

Leblon

Ipanema
Beach
General Os
statior

0 km   10
0 miles   10

Area of
main map

Museu Casa do
Pontal

BIKE

TAXI

Praia da
Barra da Tijuca

Sítio Burle
Marx

TAXI

Four Days in Rio de Janeiro

Day ❶

MORNING

Take the cable car up Sugar Loaf Mountain *(see pp16–17)* and soak up the panorama below. Tour downtown Centro, starting at **Praça XV** *(see pp28–9)* to visit its historic sights, such as the **Paço Imperial** *(see p29)*, **Museu Histórico Nacional** *(see pp26–7)*, or the **Mosteiro de São Bento** *(see pp18–19)*.

The lovely, Art Nouveau Confeitaria Colombo – a century-old pastry house.

AFTERNOON

Have a chilled *agua de coco* (coconut water) on **Ipanema Beach** *(see pp32–3)* then visit the magnificent **Fundação Eva Klabin** *(see p77)* followed by a drink at a bar overlooking **Lagoa Rodrigo de Freitas** *(see p80)*.

Day ❷

MORNING

Take the first train up to **Corcovado** *(see pp12–13)* and watch the early-morning sun bathe the city below.

AFTERNOON

Explore the cobbled lanes of **Santa Teresa** then hit the streets of **Lapa** *(see pp82–5)*, spending the evening in its vibrant bars and *samba* clubs.

Day ❸

MORNING

Go for a hike around the **Parque Nacional da Tijuca** *(see pp14–15)* and have a picnic lunch at one of its *mirantes* (lookout points).

AFTERNOON

Wander the trails of the **Jardim Botânico** *(see pp24–5)* and go for tea at the **Confeitaria Colombo** *(see p52)*. Spend the evening in chic **Leblon** *(see pp32–3)*.

Day ❹

MORNING

Explore the booming western districts by riding a hired bicycle along **Barra da Tijuca's** *(see p99)* seafront, admiring surfers on its Atlantic breakers.

AFTERNOON

Choose between one of Barra's museums: the lush **Sítio Roberto Burle Marx** *(see p98)* or the quirky **Museu Casa do Pontal** *(see p97)*.

Map labels

Mosteiro de São Bento

SAÚDE

Praça XV

CENTRO

Museu Nacional de Belas Artes

Museu Histórico Nacional

Cinelândia station

Lapa

LAPA

TRAM

GLÓRIA

CATETE

METRO

Largo do Machado station

FLAMENGO

tafogo station

FOGO

URCA

Sugar Loaf Mountain

CABLE CAR

l Arcoverde station

LEME

METRO

TAXI

Copacabana Beach

Avenida Atlântica

OPACABANA

Confeitaria Colombo

0 km   1
0 miles   1

Key

━━ Two-day itinerary
━━ Four-day itinerary

Top 10 Rio de Janeiro Highlights

Rio de Janeiro's iconic
Cristo Redentor statue

Rio de Janeiro Highlights	**10**
Corcovado	**12**
Parque Nacional da Tijuca	**14**
Sugar Loaf Mountain	**16**
Mosteiro de São Bento	**18**
Museu Nacional de Belas Artes	**20**
Jardim Botânico	**24**
Museu Histórico Nacional	**26**
Praça XV	**28**
Praia de Copacabana	**30**
Ipanema and Leblon Beachlife	**32**

🔟 Rio de Janeiro's Highlights

Rio, like its people, is warm, musical, and devoted to enjoying itself. Each neighborhood has a distinct character, and an unforgettable view of Cristo Redentor, which surveys the city with arms spread in perpetual welcome.

1 Corcovado
The Christ statue was voted one of the seven wonders of the modern world. Views from here are wonderful *(see pp12–13)*.

2 Parque Nacional da Tijuca
One of the world's largest tracts of urban rain forest, this park has abundant wildlife, waterfalls, and diverse biomes *(see pp14–15)*.

3 Sugar Loaf Mountain
This boulder-shaped mountain at the south end of Botafogo beach offers magnificent views. The summit is reached by cable car *(see pp16–17)*.

4 Mosteiro de São Bento
This Benedictine church and abbey was founded in 1590, although most of its gilt interior dates from the 1600s *(see pp18–19)*.

Museu Nacional de Belas Artes 5
The country's first art gallery displays Brazilian art from the colonial age to the late 20th century, plus works by international masters such as Rodin *(see pp20–21)*.

6 Jardim Botânico

Rio's botanical gardens, founded in 1808 by Prince Regent João, preserve nearly 8,000 species of plants. The orchids are particularly notable *(see pp24–5)*.

7 Museu Histórico Nacional

This museum explores Brazilian history from prehistoric times, with replica rock paintings from the Serra da Capivara, through to the early days of the republic *(see pp26–7)*.

8 Praça XV

This historic public square has the city's largest concentration of pre-20th-century buildings *(see pp28–9)*.

9 Praia de Copacabana

One of the world's most famous urban beaches stretches for 2.5 miles (4 km) from the Morro do Leme, at the northern end, to Arpoador in the south. This tourist hub is renowned for its New Year celebrations *(see pp30–31)*.

10 Ipanema and Leblon Beachlife

Rio's most attractive beaches, just south of Copacabana, front fashionable neighborhoods, which are a magnet for tourists *(see pp32–3)*.

Corcovado

The iconic Cristo Redentor (Christ the Redeemer) watches over Rio de Janeiro from the 2,316-ft (706-m) high Corcovado, named for the Portuguese word for hunchback. The winning design in a competition for a monument to represent the spirit of the city, it was inaugurated in 1931 and has come to symbolize Brazil. The journey to Christ's feet – through the streets of Cosme Velho and the Parque Nacional da Tijuca – is as rewarding as the panorama from the summit.

Cristo Redentor ④
Embracing the city with open arms, the magnificent 98-ft (30-m) tall statue of Jesus Christ **(right)** was designed by Brazilian Heitor da Silva Costa, and draws inspiration from Leonardo da Vinci's famous study of the human body. The structure was hauled up the mountain in pieces and took years to assemble.

② Art Deco Features
The figure **(left)** was carved from blocks of soapstone by French Art Deco sculptor Paul Landowski, who is well-known for his Art Deco statue of St. Geneviève in Paris.

⑤ The Chapel at the Base of the Statue
Underneath the figure, facing away from the sea, this small chapel is a haven of peace amid the throngs of tourists. Mass is held here daily at 11am.

① Refreshments
The bars and restaurants behind and below the statue **(below)** offer cold drinks, light meals, and welcome shade from the sun.

③ The Forest Setting
Corcovado is surrounded by the Parque Nacional da Tijuca. The views across the canopy are beautiful in the late afternoon when the setting sun burns a deep orange behind the trees.

⑥ Sunsets and Sunrises
For the classic view of Rio **(above)**, come early in the morning or late in the day when the light is soft and the sun either rises from the bay or sets behind the Floresta da Tijuca (see p14).

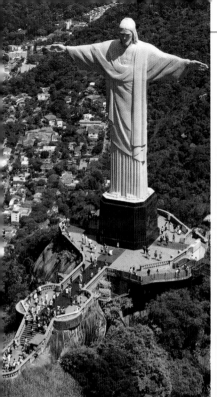

10 The Trem do Corcovado

The funicular railway (**below**) runs from Cosme Velho to the summit. Opened in 1884, it is 47 years older than the Christ statue.

A SEVENTH WONDER

In 2007, Cristo Redentor was declared one of the winners in a global poll to find the "New Seven Wonders of the World", a modern version of Greek historian Herodotus' list from the 5th century BCE. The New Open World Corporation poll is thought to have been the largest ever, with 100 million voters.

9 The Trem do Corcovado Museum

This museum (**left**) in the Cosme Velho station at the foot of Corcovado has various exhibits on the history of the railway and the Christ statue.

7 Lookout Points

There are panoramic views out over the city and Guanabara Bay from the platform at Christ's feet. The platforms behind and below the statue offer fine views of Parque Nacional da Tijuca.

8 Largo do Boticário

At the bottom of Corcovado lies this colorful square *(see p78)*. Stop by before taking the funicular railway up to the Cristo Redentor statue from the nearby station.

NEED TO KNOW

MAP M1 ▪ Rua Cosme Velho 513, Corcovado ▪ (21) 2558 1329 ▪ www.tremdocorcovado.rio

Open 8am–5pm Mon–Fri (until 6pm Sat & Sun) Funicular railway (Trem do Corcovado): weekdays US$17.70, weekends, public and school hols US$22.25; organized tour: from US$45; or taxi till Estrada das Paineiras and an authorized van thereafter; you cannot drive to the top in your own vehicle

▪ Do not walk back from Corcovado after dark. Muggings are common on the park road and the street lighting is poor.

Parque Nacional da Tijuca

This stunning national park contains the Floresta da Tijuca (Tijuca Forest), one of the world's largest urban forests. It also features the dramatic Serra de Carioca (Carioca Mountains), the impressive Pedra da Gávea monolith, and Cristo Redentor, which looms over the city from the top of Corcovado. Home to countless species of plants and animals, as well as waterfalls and springs, this peaceful forest, which covers 15 sq miles (39 sq km), is a little piece of paradise.

1 Os Esquilos
A favorite lunch spot on Sundays for wealthy Cariocas, Os Esquilos or "Squirrels" restaurant, is romantically situated under the shade of trees in the heart of this park.

3 Trails and Walks
Many trails cut through Floresta da Tijuca, the lengths of which vary. There are full-day hikes to the park's peaks, at Pedra da Gávea and Pico da Tijuca (see p46).

Lush Floresta da Tijuca

2 Hang-Gliding
A very popular hang-gliding spot **(above)**, the Pedra Bonita (another monolith) is next to Pedra da Gávea and is accessible by road and a short trail. Flights can be fixed through tour operators (see p42).

4 Cascatinha do Taunay
The most accessible of the numerous waterfalls that lie in Floresta da Tijuca can be found just off the road a few miles away from the Alto da Boa Vista park gate. Its spectacular cascades **(left)** plummet from a height of 100 ft (30 m).

5 Wildlife
Endemic wildlife in Parque Nacional da Tijuca includes primates such as the tiny tufted-eared marmoset **(above)**, as well as 200 species of birds, many of which are critically endangered.

6 Park Roads

A series of roads **(left)** run through the park, connecting the neighborhoods of Santa Teresa, Jardim Botânico, and Barra da Tijuca *(see p99)*. Route maps are available in the visitors' center.

REFORESTATION IN IMPERIAL RIO

Deforestation of Tijuca to make room for sugar and coffee plantations during the early years of colonial rule led to such bad flooding that Emperor Dom Pedro II commissioned its reforestation in 1861. It took 13 years for army major Manuel Gomes Archer and six unnamed enslaved Africans to re-plant the forest with native and introduced trees.

9 The Mayrink Chapel

The panels inside this tiny 1863 chapel are replicas of paintings by the Brazilian Modernist artist Cândido Portinari. The originals are in the Museu Nacional de Belas Artes *(see pp20–21)*.

10 Mirante Andaime Pequeno

This is another fantastic lookout point, which looms over the Jardim Botânico neighborhood. It offers sweeping vistas across emerald-green treetops to the striking Corcovado mountain and Cristo Redentor.

NEED TO KNOW

MAP D4

Visitor Center: Estrada da Cascatinha 850; Alto de Boa Vista; (21) 2492 2250; open 8am–5pm daily; www.parqueda tijuca.com.br

Os Esquilos: Estrada Barão D'Escragnole, Alto da Boa Vista, Tijuca; (21) 2492 2197; open noon–5pm Sat & Sun

■ It easy to get lost in the park, so it is best to come on a tour or hire a guide. Try Rio Hiking *(www.riohiking.com.br)*.

■ Bring water and a snack; there are few restaurants in the park.

7 Pedra da Gávea

Said to be the world's largest coastal monolith, this granite boulder on the forest's edge overlooks Rio's suburbs.

8 Mirante Dona Marta

This lookout **(above)**, which is perched above the beachfront neighborhood of Botafogo *(see p40)*, boasts superb views of the Sugar Loaf *(see pp16–17)*. Note that this area is not safe to visit after dark.

TOP10 ⭐ Sugar Loaf Mountain

None of Rio's magnificent views are more breathtaking than those from the top of the 1,312-ft (400-m) high granite and quartz Pão de Açúcar (Sugar Loaf) at the mouth of Guanabara Bay. Marmosets, tanagers, and myriad birds are a common sight on the trails that run around the monolith's summit. Visit early in the day or after rain for the clearest views from here and its majestic neighbor – Morro da Urca.

3 Morro da Urca
From Corcovado, Sugar Loaf Mountain resembles a sphinx **(left)**, whose body is made up of Morro da Urca – a separate, lower boulder mountain with a flat summit.

4 Bars and Cafés
Set in the shade of trees, bars and cafés around the Sugar Loaf offer refreshment and respite from the sun.

5 Helicopter Tours
Flights **(right)** over the triumvirate of Sugar Loaf, Corcovado, and Estádio do Maracanã (see p39) are run by Helisight (see p111) and leave from Morro da Urca and Lagoa Rodrigo de Freitas (see p76).

1 Rock Climbing
Tour agencies offer rock-climbing trips (see p43) suitable for both experienced and novice climbers. Rio's stunning views make not looking down a challenge.

2 The Path Up Morro da Urca
The Pista Claúdio Coutinho starts from the suburb of Urca, next to Praia Vermelha, and connects to a trail up to the summit of Morro da Urca (see p73). Allow at least one hour for the walk and take plenty of water with you.

6 Walks at the Summit
Winding trails **(left)** meander around the summit of the Sugar Loaf. Walks lead through shady forests abundant with tropical birds and butterflies, and lead to a multitude of lookout points that offer views across the city.

⑦ The Sugar Loaf

The spectacular Sugar Loaf **(below)** is one of the highest points above sea level in Rio de Janeiro and is reachable by cable car from Morro da Urca. The first recorded solo climb of the Sugar Loaf was made by British nanny Henrietta Carstairs in 1817.

⑩ The Cable Car

Offering convenient access for people of all levels of fitness, the cable car **(above)** runs from the suburb of Urca to the summit of the Sugar Loaf via Morro da Urca. Those looking for a hike can also walk up to the summit via a trail.

PÃO DE AÇÚCAR

The name Sugar Loaf is derived from the rock's shape, which resembles the conical clay molds once used to refine sugar. The Indigenous Tupi Guarani people, however, referred to it as *Pau-nh-acqua* (high, pointed, or isolated hill).

⑧ Views of the City

There is a dramatic, 360-degree view **(below)** out over Rio, Guanabara Bay, and the surrounding rain forest-covered mountains from a variety of lookout points located on both Morro da Urca and Sugar Loaf Mountain.

⑨ Wildlife

Tufted-eared marmosets and various species of rare birds, including the seven-colored tanager, are a common sight on the Sugar Loaf. The trees are adorned with bromeliads, orchids, and other flora.

NEED TO KNOW

MAP J4 ■ Av Pasteur 520, Urca ■ Cable cars leave from Urca every 20 minutes ■ www. bondinho.com.br/en

Open 8am–8pm (last adm 6:30pm)

Adm US$29

....

■ Allow three hours to see both the Sugar Loaf and Morro da Urca.

■ There are cafés on both hills, and drinks and snacks are available from the cable car station in Urca.

TOP 10 ⭐ Mosteiro de São Bento

The Benedictines, the first religious order to establish itself firmly in Brazil, founded this magnificent hilltop monastery and church in 1590. Dedicated to Our Lady of Montserrat, one of the Black Madonnas of Europe, it has richly decorated interiors that date from the 18th century – the formative years of Brazilian Baroque. The interior took almost 70 years to complete and was the life work of a series of artists, notably Benedictine monk Frei Domingos da Conceição (1643–1718).

Facade ①
The unadorned, sober facade of the monastery (right), with its whitewashed plaster, raw stone masonry, and squat geometrical towers, contrasts starkly with the gilded opulence of the interior.

③ Baroque Doors
The elaborately carved Baroque doors that provide access to the nave are also considered to be the work of Frei Domingos da Conceição. They are thought to have been carved in the period between 1699 and the monk's death in 1718.

④ Candelabras
The church was originally illuminated by candles held in ornate candelabras cast from silver by the artist Mestre Valentim. The most impressive of these still sit next to the altarpiece.

② Statue of St. Scholastica
A glorious work by sculptor Frei Domingos da Conceição, this intricately carved statue (above) depicts St. Scholastica, who was the twin sister of St. Benedict. The saint's name stands for "she who is devoted to theological study."

⑤ Paintings by Frei Ricardo Pilar
The painting *Christ of the Martyrs* by the German Benedictine monk Ricardo Pilar dates from 1690 and is the finest of all his paintings on display in the church.

NEED TO KNOW

MAP W1 ■ Rua Dom Gerardo 68, Centro
■ (21) 2206 8100
■ www.mosteirode saobentorio.org.br

Open 6:30am–6:30pm daily

■ Photography of any kind is not permitted in the church.

■ There are no drinks available at the monastery, so be sure to carry water.

6 Chapel of the Santíssimo

This chapel is the most sacred part of the church. It preserves the consecrated host – bread that Catholics believe to be the body of Christ – and has lavish Rococo features, such as the gilded carvings and a burnished sacred heart **(left)**.

ST. BENEDICT

St. Benedict of Nursia, the founder of Western monasticism, was a Roman noble who left home to live as a hermit. Inspired by his saintliness, the community of an abbey requested St. Benedict to be their leader. He later founded a monastery, where he wrote the Rule of the Benedictine Order.

9 The Library

The monastery's library **(below)** preserves one of the finest collections of ancient religious books in Brazil. It is open only to those members of the public who have requested permission in writing from the abbot.

7 Statue of St. Benedict

Regarded as one of the crowning achievements of Baroque in Rio de Janeiro, this elaborate statue of the founder of the Benedictine order is located at the back of the church **(above)**, and forms a part of the beautiful altarpiece.

10 Statue of Our Lady of Montserrat

This statue of the patron saint of the church was also created by Frei Domingos da Conceição. There are many other paintings of the patron saint adorning the walls of the church and monastery.

8 Gilded Ornamentation

The Brazilian Baroque interior of the church is considered the most ornate in Rio, with almost every square inch richly decorated with gold leaf **(left)**.

TOP 10 ★ Museu Nacional de Belas Artes

Housing the most comprehensive collection of Brazilian art in the country, the National Museum of Fine Arts was established in 1937 in the former Brazilian Academy of Fine Arts building. The collection comprises close to 70,000 pieces, including fine, decorative, and popular art. The majority of works are Brazilian from the 17th to the 20th centuries. A small number are foreign, predominantly from Europe.

3 The Sculpture Gallery

A corridor lined with statues looking out on to a central space, this gallery **(right)** houses works that include classical reproductions and original pieces by artists such as Rodin and Brecheret.

4 Portadora de Perfumes

Victor Brecheret, Brazil's most highly respected sculptor, was one of Latin America's foremost practitioners of Art Deco. His work can be seen across Brazil. *Portadora de Perfumes* was cast from bronze in 1923.

1 Almeida's Arrufos

Avant-garde painter Belmiro de Almeida learned cutting-edge styles in Europe in the 1880s. *Arrufos* **(above)**, painted in 1887, is considered his masterpiece.

5 Batalha do Avaí

Brazilian painter Pedro Américo's epic work, a majestic mock-European canvas, depicts the decisive battle of the 1868 war between Paraguay and the triple alliance of Uruguay, Argentina, and Brazil.

6 Pernambuco Landscapes

Some of the earliest Brazilian landscapes were painted in the 17th century by expatriate artists in Dutch-occupied Pernambuco. The most famous of these artists was Franz Post.

2 Primeira Missa no Brasil

Victor Meirelles's 1861 painting **(above)**, fully restored in 2007, depicts the moment the Portuguese first recited mass on Brazilian soil.

7 Works by Tarsila do Amaral

Do Amaral and her husband, Oswald de Andrade, defined the first distinctly Brazilian approach to art, which they termed *antropofagismo*. **(left)** This involved adapting Western themes to Brazilian contexts.

9 European Engravings

One of the museum's collections preserves an important archive of engravings and sketches by a number of famous European painters and illustrators including Goya, Doré, and Picasso.

10 Café by Portinari

Cândido Portinari, a graduate of Rio's Escola Nacional de Belas Artes, was one of Brazil's most influential Modernist painters. His work falls into two periods: *Café* **(below)** is an example of Social Realism and draws inspiration from Mexican muralists such as Diego Rivera, while most of his other work is Expressionistic.

NEED TO KNOW

MAP X3 ■ Av Rio Branco 199, Centro
■ (21) 3299 0600
■ www.mnba.gov.br

Open 10am–6pm Tue–Fri, noon–5pm Sat, Sun & hols (partially closed for renovation until spring 2024)

Adm US$2 (free on Sun)

■ It is better to visit in the afternoon when it's hot outside and the gallery is less busy.

■ The Theatro Municipal, across Avenida Rio Branco in Cinelândia, has an excellent café *(see p69)*.

8 Rodin's Meditação Sem Braço

The Modernist sculptor's tortured *Meditação Sem Braço* (Meditation without Arms) was acquired by Fundação Roberto Marinho.

Following pages The statue of Cristo Redentor gazes out over the city and bay

TOP 10 ⭐ Jardim Botânico

Tucked away behind Lagoa Rodrigo de Freitas and Ipanema beach, Rio's shady Jardim Botânico offers a haven from the urban rush. Founded by Prince Regent João in 1808 as a repository for imported plants to become acclimatized to the tropics, the gardens were opened to the public after the Proclamation of the Republic in 1889. Plants are grouped in distinct areas linked by gravel paths and interspersed with streams and waterfalls. The gardens lend their name to the neighborhood, which has excellent restaurants and nightlife.

① Views of Corcovado

The gardens boast wonderful views of Corcovado *(see pp12–13)*, which is visible in the distance through the trees. The ideal time for taking photographs is in the late afternoon, when visitors start to leave and the light is at its best.

③ The Arboretum

The garden is home to some 8,000 plant species, including the many native Brazilian trees in the arboretum.

② The Avenue of Palms

The stately Avenue of Palms **(above)** is located in the center of the gardens close to a magnificent classical fountain. It is lined with 40-ft (13-m) tall palms, which were planted at the time the gardens were established.

④ Fountains

These lush gardens are relatively quiet, except for the soothing tinkle of running water from the 19th-century fountains **(right)** that pepper the grounds. This, and the incessant birdsong, offers a welcome break from the noisy streets.

8 Museu Casa dos Pilões

This simple, whitewashed cottage **(left)**, hidden away near the Orquidarium, was once the center for grinding saltpeter, charcoal, and sulfur into gunpowder for the 1808 Royal Rio de Janeiro Gunpowder Factory, which is also in the garden.

5 The Café Botânico

Cariocas visit Jardim Botânico not just to enjoy the stunningly diverse plant life, but also to enjoy a coffee or light lunch in the open-air café, next to the cactus gardens.

9 The Orquidarium

This part of the garden is home to some of the world's most rare orchids, including the famous *Cattleya* **(below)**. Some 1,000 tropical orchids are cultivated and preserved here.

6 Giant Amazon Lilies

The world's largest waterlilies **(left)**, the *Victoria amazonica* or *Victoria regia* are cultivated on ponds in the gardens. Identified in the 19th century, the lily was named for British monarch Queen Victoria.

A BOTANICAL ARK

Brazil has approximately 166 million hectares (411 million acres) of nature preserves, which amounts to 18 per cent of the continental territory and 26 per cent of the marine area. According to botanists, this is too little to ensure the protection of many vulnerable ecosystems. Botanical gardens play a crucial role in plant conservation, preserving many rare species.

NEED TO KNOW

MAP L3 ■ Rua Jardim Botânico 1008 ■ (21) 3874 1808 ■ Bus 309 from the center, 410 and 309 from Glória and Lapa, or 109, 584 from Copacabana and Ipanema ■ www.jbrj. gov.br

Open 8am–5pm daily

Adm US$13

■ The best time to see birds and marmosets is in the early morning during the week, when visitor numbers are low.

7 Bird-Watching

The gardens offer some of the best urban bird-watching in Brazil. Masked water tyrants **(above)**, woodnymphs, foliage-gleaners, parakeets, woodcreepers, and aplomado falcons are the easiest to spot.

10 The Jardim dos Beija-Flores

This pretty hummingbird garden has been planted with hundreds of brightly colored flowering plants that attract numerous species of butterflies, such as the Blue Morpho, as well as more than 20 different species of hummingbird.

🟊 **Museu Histórico Nacional**

One of Rio's best museums is devoted to the history of Brazil. Exhibits include paintings, sculptures, photographs and maps, among other artifacts. Galleries focus on Indigenous tribes, while the colonial, imperial, and republican eras are also well represented. Visitors can see a replica of the ancient rock paintings from Serra da Capivara in Northeast Brazil, claimed to be the oldest record of human presence in South America.

5 Statue of Dom Pedro II

This romanticized statue by a Carioca sculptor was first exhibited at the 1867 Paris Exhibition and portrays Emperor Dom Pedro II riding a horse.

1 Citizenship in Construction

Focusing on political, civil, and social rights from 1889 to the present, this exhibition **(above)** displays paintings of leading historical figures and events, as well as videos of 20th-century life in Brazil.

4 Building the Nation

These galleries chart Brazil's path to independence, with exhibits on the War of the Triple Alliance, the abolition of slavery, the social uprising leading to the exile of the Portuguese royal family, and the 1889 Proclamation of the Republic.

2 Portuguese Around the World

This area of the museum covers 400 years of history, from the Portuguese colonization of Brazil, through the gold and diamond booms, to the 1822 Proclamation of Independence.

3 Imperial Thrones

The thrones displayed at the museum **(right)** were the seats of state, used for grand occasions by the Portuguese exiled king, João VI, and by the Brazilian Emperors Dom Pedro I and Pedro II.

NEED TO KNOW

MAP Y3 ■ Praça Marechal Âncora, Centro
■ (21) 3299 0324 ■ mhn. museus.gov.br

Open 10am–5pm Wed–Fri, 1–5pm Sat & Sun

■ The museum can be visited on the way to or from Praça XV *(see pp28–9)*.

■ Set aside three hours or more to explore the museum fully.

■ The museum has an excellent café on the first floor.

8 Farmácia Teixeira Novaes

A full-scale, mood-lit reproduction of an 18th-century Rio de Janeiro apothecary shop **(left)**, this exhibit also includes a replica of the back office and laboratory.

THE BUILDING

Museu Histórico Nacional is housed in a former arsenal and retains a wall from the city's first fort – a reminder of Rio's colonial past. The city center was once as grand as that of Buenos Aires, but the hill, the fort, and much of Portuguese Rio were demolished post independence in order to break away from its colonial history.

6 Royal Carriages

As the only South American country to have had a monarchy, Brazil retains many vestiges of its royal past. The museum houses the ornate carriages **(above)** of both Emperor Dom Pedro II and Empress Teresa Christina.

9 Pátio dos Canhões

This atrium is filled with rusting cannons, many of which date to the colonial period. Others come from the UK and France.

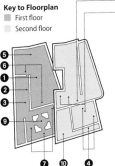

7 Temporary Galleries

Some of Rio's most exciting visiting shows, featuring both local and international works, are displayed here. Information about the exhibitions can be found on the museum's website.

Museu Histórico Nacional

Key to Floorplan
First floor
Second floor

10 Combate Naval do Riachuelo

Victor Meirelles' grand and sweeping oil on canvas, in the spirit of the European Romantics, idealizes Brazil's campaign against Paraguay in the War of the Triple Alliance, also known as the Great War.

TOP 10 ★ Praça XV

Praça XV was the first area to develop during the 18th century Minas Gerais gold rush. The square became a trading center, and trade still takes place here in the market next to Rua 1 de Março. It also served as the center of Brazil's political power under the Portuguese. Today, Praça XV is dotted with historical buildings and streets. The 1980s restoration of Paço Imperial catalyzed the return of culture to the city center. A further facelift was given to the area for the 2016 Olympic Games.

1 Exhibition Galleries

Today, the Paço Imperial serves as a cultural center, hosting some of Rio's best small exhibitions, many devoted to the nation's history and cultural life.

2 Igreja Santa Cruz dos Militares

This was one of Rio de Janeiro's grandest churches **(below)** when it was built in the 17th century. Badly damaged in a fire in 1923, it was restored and still retains a few original details attributed to the celebrated sculptor Mestre Valentim, who created its carvings.

3 Estação das Barcas

With its prominent clock and faux-Baroque architecture, this boat station **(above)** was the hub of Brazil's international trade – most of which came through Rio.

4 Palácio Tiradentes

This 1920s palace is the seat of the Legislative Assembly of the State of Rio de Janeiro. A statue of Tiradentes – the first Brazilian to rebel against the Portuguese – stands in front of the building.

5 Igreja de Nossa Senhora do Carmo da Antiga Sé

Known as the Old Cathedral, this church's modest exterior encloses a beautiful interior with a Rococo nave, ceiling panels, and wall carvings.

Praça XV

6 Ferry Dock

The Portuguese royal family disembarked just to the west of this spot when they arrived here in 1808. Today, ferries leave from the dock for Niterói, across the bay.

7 Chafariz do Mestre Valentim

This public drinking fountain **(left)** was designed in 1789 by Mestre Valentim, one of the city's most important Baroque artists. It was intended for use by sailors whose boats were moored on the nearby quays.

QUEEN MARIA

The Faculdade Cândido Mendes at Praça XV 101, formerly a Carmelite convent, was used to incarcerate Portugal's Queen Maria, who was known to be mentally ill. Her son, João (later King João VI), ruled in her stead as Regent until her death in 1816.

10 Igreja da Ordem Terceira de Nossa Senhora do Monte do Carmo

Situated next to the Old Cathedral, this 18th-century church boasts an opulent interior **(left)** covered in gilt carvings, many by Mestre Valentim.

NEED TO KNOW

MAP X2

Igreja Santa Cruz dos Militares: Rua 1 de Março 36

Palácio Tiradentes: Rua Primeiro de Março s/n; open 10am–5pm Mon–Sat, noon–5pm Sun & hols

Igreja de Nossa Senhora do Carmo da Antiga Sé: Rua 1 de Março; open 7am–4pm Mon–Fri, 9:30am–12:30pm Sat, 9am–1pm Sun (mass: 8am Mon–Fri, 11am Sun)

Paço Imperial and Exhibition Galleries: Praça XV 48; open noon–6pm Tue–Fri (until 5pm Sat & Sun)

Igreja da Ordem Terceira de Nossa Senhora do Monte do Carmo: Rua Primeiro de Março s/n; open 8am–4pm Mon–Fri (until 11am Sat)

- On Sundays avoid the empty streets around the square.

8 Paço Imperial

This modest colonial building was built in 1743 as the seat of government. When the Portuguese royal family arrived in Brazil in 1808, a third floor was added and the building became the Imperial Palace.

9 Travessa do Comércio

This charming pedestrian street **(left)** is lined with several bars and restaurants. Carmen Miranda lived in a house in this alley as a young girl.

TOP 10 Praia de Copacabana

One of Rio's most celebrated beaches, Copacabana stretches from the Morro do Leme in the northeast to the Arpoador in the southwest. It is a year-round tourist hub, famed for its New Year's Eve celebrations. When a tunnel connected the area with Botafogo in 1892, Copacabana was an unspoilt bay with picturesque dunes. By the time the Copacabana Palace hotel was built, the neighborhood had more than 30,000 residents. Today, it is one of the most densely populated areas in the world.

1 Forte Duque de Caxias
This 18th-century fort is also called Forte do Leme. A steep climb from the beach, it is named for the general who fought in the 1868 War of the Triple Alliance. The views **(left)** are spectacular.

2 Copacabana Palace
Many famous visitors have stayed at this grand Art Deco hotel *(see p112)*. Pictures of past celebrity guests are displayed on the second floor.

3 New Year's Eve
Copacabana hosts Rio's biggest New Year's Eve party, when as many as 2 million people gather to listen to live music concerts and watch the midnight fireworks.

4 Mosaic Pavements
Copacabana's unique black-and-white wave-patterned pavements form a beachfront promenade that is typically Portuguese in style. They were designed by Brazilian landscape architect Roberto Burle Marx.

5 Beach Soccer
The beach, which is several times wider than a soccer field is long, is the place where *favela* kids have long honed their soccer skills.

6 Forte de Copacabana
This fort **(below)** at the southern end affords great views. A museum here charts the history of the army in Brazil from colonial times.

NEED TO KNOW
MAP Q5–R3

■ The beach is floodlit all night, but it is best avoided after dark as criminals often target the area.

■ On Sundays, the road closest to the beach is closed to traffic most of the day, so this is a particularly good day for cycling and jogging along the beachside track that leads west to Barra da Tijuca.

■ There are bicycle hire stands along the beach.

■ The beach is lined with numerous cafés and stalls selling cold, fresh coconut water.

WHAT'S IN A NAME?

Copacabana takes its name from a Bolivian town on the shores of Lake Titicaca, where stood an effigy of Our Lady of Copacabana, believed to bring luck to sailors. The captain of a Spanish galleon thought he was saved from shipwreck by praying to Her, and built a chapel in Her honor near the Arpoador Rocks. This chapel gave the area and beach their name.

⑩ Morro do Leme

Copacabana is marked by a monolith – the Morro do Leme **(above)** – which is partially covered with forest. Take the trails up the hill at weekends when guards monitor the entrance.

⑦ Copacabana and Leme Neighborhoods

Copacabana beach **(above)** fronts two neighborhoods – Leme and Copacabana itself. The area is filled with hotels, and vibrant restaurants, bars, and shops.

⑧ Beach Vendors

Beer, snacks like the *biscoito globo*, sun umbrellas, *cangas*, flip-flops, and massages are all offered by itinerant beach vendors, who walk along the beach from dawn to dusk proffering their wares.

⑨ Fishers

In the late 19th century, southern Copacabana was home only to a fort and a tiny fishing community, whose descendants own the colorful fishing boats **(above)** that sit on the sand next to Forte de Copacabana.

TOP 10 ⭐ Ipanema and Leblon Beachlife

Ipanema and its extension farther south, Leblon, are urban Rio's most beautiful, fashionable, and secure beaches. Most tourists make their base at the two wealthy neighborhoods located behind their eponymous beaches, where chic boutiques and glamorous restaurants line the streets. Neighboring Copacabana, the Jardim Botânico, Gávea, and Corcovada, are easily reached from here.

1 Cycling and Running Tracks

For health-conscious visitors looking for more than sunbathing and lounging on the sand, there are 2-mile- (3.5-km-) long cycling and running tracks **(right)** along the entire length of both beaches.

2 Beach Exercise

Alongside a multitude of home-grown beach sports, exercising on the sand in these body-conscious neighborhoods is a vanity fair. A popular spot for this is around the pull-up bars in front of Rua Farme de Amoedo, which serves as a posing ground for fitness enthusiasts.

3 Farme Beach

This stretch, between Postos 8 and 9, is the favorite daytime haunt for Rio's LGBTQ+ community. Look for the rainbow flags **(below)**, displayed with pride by beach vendors.

4 Beach Volleyball and Futevolei

Beach volleyball is a favorite pastime and the national women's team practice on Ipanema. *Futevolei* (footvolley) is played entirely with the feet and head *(see p45)*.

5 Beachwear

The essential Ipanema and Leblon beach kit comprises a *tanga* and *canga* (bikini and sarong) for women, and a *sunga* (speedos) for men. Buy these items, along with sunglasses and other essentials, from the vendors *(see p54)* behind the beach.

6 Children's Play Areas

There are kids' play areas **(above)** at the Baixo Bebê kiosk *(see p48)* on Leblon beach and in Praça Nossa Senhora da Paz, behind Ipanema beach.

8 Beachside Cafés

The beachside kiosks that line Ipanema and Leblon beaches serve snacks, drinks, and delicious ice-cold coconut water, drunk straight from the coconut shell. The cafés also offer shade from the sun.

Cariocas relax in the sun on Ipanema Beach

9 Sand Sculptures

Carioca artists create elaborate fantasy castles and sculptures **(above)** from Ipanema's fine sand. Look out for them right next to the running tracks.

NEED TO KNOW

Ipanema: **MAP M6–N6**
Leblon: **MAP L6**

- Avoid walking on the beach after dark.
- Energy drinks can be bought from juice bars throughout Ipanema and Leblon.

7 Postos

These concrete bunkers on the beach are more than lifeguard stations – social status is reflected by the location of your towel on the beach. The closer you are to the most fashionable position, near Posto Nove (9) in Ipanema, the higher your status.

10 Beach Massage

Massages on make-shift couches and chairs have been offered on Ipanema and Leblon for decades. These tend to be of a very high standard and are reasonably priced.

The Top 10 of Everything

Oscar Niemeyer's stunning Museu de
Arte Contemporânea de Niterói

Moments in History	36	Restaurants	52
Museums and Art Galleries	38	Shopping	54
Beaches	40	Rio de Janeiro for Free	56
Outdoor Activities	42	Carnaval Parades and Balls	58
Soccer	44	Festivals and Shows	60
Off the Beaten Path	46		
Activities for Children	48		
Bars and Nightclubs	50		

🔟 Moments in History

A sketch by explorer Paul Macroy depicting river-faring Indigenous people

1 The First Brazilians

Brazil's first inhabitants are believed to have traveled across temporary land bridges that linked Asia and America at the Bering Straits. They then traveled south through the Americas between 40,000 and 12,000 years ago.

2 Portuguese Land in Rio

On January 1, 1502, the Portuguese explorer Gaspar de Lemos arrived in Guanabara Bay – which he mistakenly named Rio de Janeiro (January River) – and he built a small fort to claim the bay for Portugal. But hostile confrontations with the Indigenous Tamoio people led the Portuguese to establish their colony elsewhere in Brazil.

3 The French Arrive

In 1555, France sent a fleet of ships under Admiral Nicolas Durand de Villegagnon to Rio, where they claimed a tiny island in Guanabara Bay. The French treated the Tamoios far better than the Portuguese had done and succeeded in forging a military alliance with them.

4 The Portuguese Defeat the French–Tamoio Alliance

The Portuguese returned to Rio and, with various Indigenous groups, fought numerous battles against the French–Tamoio Alliance, eventually defeating it on January 20, 1567.

5 The Portuguese Royal Court Moves to Rio

In November 1807, the Portuguese royal family fled Napoleon. Their fleet comprised some 40 ships, packed with 15,000 members of the Portuguese court and government, and Rio became the capital of Portugal.

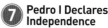

King Dom João VI

6 The French Cultural Mission

In 1816, King Dom João VI of Portugal invited the French to introduce European culture to Rio (see p21) by bringing in their styles of architecture, art, and music.

7 Pedro I Declares Independence

King Dom João VI returned to Portugal in 1821, leaving his

son Pedro as Prince Regent in Brazil. Pedro declared independence from Portugal the following year, and crowned himself Emperor Dom Pedro I. He and his son, Pedro II, ruled over the new country for the next 67 years.

8 Brazil Becomes a Republic

The republican movement of 1870 was provoked by general discontent over high taxes and the movement toward the abolition of slavery. On November 15, 1889, Emperor Dom Pedro II was overthrown and the republic was proclaimed by Marechal Deodoro da Fonseca.

Emperor Dom Pedro II

9 The Capital Moves from Rio to Brasilia

Rio de Janeiro was replaced by Brasilia as capital of Brazil in 1960. This change was overseen by President Juscelino Kubitschek and three Modernist architects, Lúcio Costa, Oscar Niemeyer (see p72), and Roberto Burle Marx.

10 Rio Hosts the FIFA World Cup and Olympics

In 2014 Brazil hosted the FIFA World Cup, the final being played at Rio's Maracanã stadium. Rio later hosted the Olympics in 2016, which were a huge success. The games were mostly held in the suburb of Barra de Tijuca.

TOP 10 HISTORICAL FIGURES

Chief Cunhambebe

1 Chief Cunhambebe
The powerful chief of the Tamoios, who almost defeated the Portuguese.

2 Gaspar de Lemos
The first European to see Rio was also present when Álvares Cabral reached Brazil in 1500.

3 Nicholas de Villegagnon
The Frenchman responsible for claiming an island in Guanabara Bay and forging alliances with the Tamoios.

4 Mem de Sá
One of Portugal's most ruthless and effective generals, Mem de Sá founded Rio along with his 17-year-old nephew, Estácio, in 1565.

5 João VI of Portugal
This Regent fled Portugal in 1808, founded imperial Brazil, and later became King João VI.

6 Emperor Dom Pedro I
Son of João VI, declarer of independence, and the first emperor of free Brazil.

7 Emperor Dom Pedro II
Pedro I's son, who helped abolish slavery and oversaw the start of industrialization.

8 Marechal Deodoro da Fonseca
The soldier who overthrew Pedro II declared Brazil a republic in 1889 and became its first president.

9 Getúlio Vargas
President from 1930 to 1945 and again from 1951 to his suicide in 1954. He copied the fascist politics of Europe.

10 Juscelino Kubitschek
Promising 50 years of progress in five, this president oversaw economic growth from 1956 to 1961, but finally bankrupted Brazil.

🔟 Museums and Art Galleries

Oscar Niemeyer's iconic **Museu de Arte Contemporânea de Niterói**

1 Museu de Arte Contemporânea de Niterói (MAC)

MAP C5 ▪ Mirante da Boa Viagem s/n, Boa Viagem, Niterói ▪ (21) 2620 2481 ▪ Open 10am–6pm Tue–Sun ▪ Adm (free on Wed) ▪ www.culturaniteroi.com.br/macniteroi

Contemporary Brazilian art is on display at this museum, housed in an iconic building designed by Oscar Niemeyer. The concrete spheroid structure sits at the end of a rocky promontory that juts into Guanabara Bay, and the interior is accessed via a long red ramp.

2 Museu Histórico Nacional

Housed in a colonial building that served as an arsenal till the 1920s, this fascinating museum *(see pp26–7)* charts Brazilian history.

3 Museu da República

MAP H3 ▪ Palácio do Catete, Rua do Catete 153 ▪ (21) 2127 0324 ▪ Open 10am–5pm Tue–Fri, 11am–5pm Sat, Sun & hols ▪ Adm

This Baroque palace, now a museum, was the site of the death of Brazil's most influential statesman. President Vargas *(see p37)* died by suicide in his bedroom here in 1954. Exhibited items include his nightshirt, with the bullet hole in the breast.

4 Museu Nacional de Belas Artes

This museum *(see pp20–21)* holds the largest collection of Brazilian art in the country, dating from colonial times through to the 21st century. International pieces are also on display here.

5 Museu do Amanhã

Set in an impressive, futuristic building, the dynamic "Museum of Tomorrow" *(see p66)* features exhibits on physics, cosmology and biology, among other topics. The collection shows how human life is a product of the cosmos and has itself become part of the earth's geology. The IRIS+ feature here allows visitors to actively engage with the exhibits and even pose questions using an artificial intelligence app.

The striking **Museu do Amanhã**

6 Estádio do Maracanã

MAP E2 ▪ Rua Professor Eurico Rabelo ▪ (21) 98341 1949 ▪ Open 9am–4pm daily (guided tours only, every 30 mins)

The pavement outside Brazil's largest soccer stadium is covered in footprints made by star players, including Pelé. A gallery dedicated to soccer greats is inside the stadium.

7 Museu de Arte Moderna (MAM)

MAP X4 ▪ Av Infante Dom Henrique 85, Parque do Flamengo ▪ (21) 3883 5611 ▪ Open 10am–6pm Thu–Sat (from 11am Sun & hols) ▪ Adm (free on Wed) ▪ www.mamrio.org.br

Housed in a modernist building on V-shaped stilts, this museum features works by local artists such as Tarsila

Museu de Arte Moderna exterior

do Amaral and Cândido Portinari, as well as international artists.

8 Sambódromo

MAP T4 ▪ Rua Marquês de Sapucaí, Praça Onze, Centro ▪ (21) 2240 9589 ▪ www.sambadrome.com ▪ Adm (Samba Museum free adm, open daily except during Carnaval)

Designed by Oscar Niemeyer and believed to be the birthplace of *samba*, this stadium hosts Carnaval parades. Inside, the Samba Museum displays costumes, musical instruments, and memorabilia from previous parades.

9 Museu Nacional

MAP E1 ▪ Quinta da Boa Vista s/n, São Cristóvão ▪ (21) 3938 1100 ▪ Closed to public until 2027 ▪ Adm ▪ www.museunacional.ufrj.br

A diverse collection of items, including the largest meteorite to fall in Brazil, dinosaur bones, and mummies, are preserved here. The building is undergoing renovation to undo the damage caused by a fire in 2018.

10 Ilha Fiscal

MAP J1 ▪ Rua Dom Manuel 15, Praça XV, Centro ▪ (21) 2233 9165 ▪ Tours: Thu–Sun & hols; hours vary, call ahead ▪ Adm

This Neo-Gothic folly was once a 19th-century royal pleasure palace that hosted masked balls that later evolved into Carnaval. It now houses a museum of Brazilian culture.

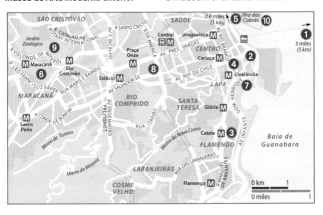

🔟 Beaches

1 Ipanema and Leblon
These two contiguous neighborhoods *(see pp32–3)* have the cleanest, safest, and most beautiful beaches in the city, and are the favorite playgrounds of Rio de Janeiro's upper-middle class.

2 Copacabana
From the 1930s to the 1970s, this fine, broad beach *(see pp30–31)* was the trendy place to lay a towel in the city. Since the 1980s, it has grown a little tawdry, especially at night. Sunbathing is best in front of the Copacabana Palace hotel.

3 Charitas
MAP C5

Cariocas are fond of saying that the best thing about Niterói – the city across Guanabara Bay – is its views of Rio. None are better than those from Charitas in the afternoon, when Corcovado and the Sugar Loaf are silhouetted against the setting sun.

4 Botafogo
MAP S1

The Sugar Loaf *(see pp16–17)* sits at the southern end of this perfectly rounded cove, which lies between Copacabana and Centro, at the mouth of the bay. It was a popular swimming spot until the 1960s, when pollution made bathing inadvisable.

São Conrado and Pedra da Gávea

5 São Conrado
This beach *(see p99)*, which is a landing point for hang-gliders, has long been popular with local television celebrities, many of whom have expensive apartments in the fortified tower blocks that stand between the sea and the city's largest *favela*, Rocinha *(see p78)*.

6 Barra da Tijuca
Rio's largest beach *(see p97)*, Barra da Tijuca is 11 miles (18 km) long and has both crowded as well as isolated stretches. It is a favorite with surfers, windsurfers, and fishing enthusiasts. The suburb, known for its many wealthy and famous residents, is characterized by long avenues, apartment blocks, and shopping malls.

7 Arpoador
MAP P6

This beach around the rocky headland at the southern end of Copacabana features cafés, coconut

The sun-kissed Botafogo beach

stalls, and juice bars where *Cariocas* hang out. Strong waves make it popular with surfers but the rocks are unsafe after dark.

8 Recreio dos Bandeirantes
MAP A6

Despite being very built up, Recreio dos Bandeirantes is a peaceful suburb. The long, straight beach here is pounded by powerful waves, making it a good surf spot.

9 Grumari
MAP A6

Surfers head to this beach at Rio's southern end beyond Barra da Tijuca *(see p97)*. The clean waters here are also the coolest in the city. There is a powerful undertow, however, which makes it unsuitable for swimming.

10 Flamengo
MAP Y6

This stretch of pearl-white sand is the prettiest of all the Guanabara Bay beaches and affords wonderful views of the bay and the Sugar Loaf. The water is now far too dirty for swimming and the beach itself is unsafe after dark. The bay is best enjoyed by boat tour; views of Rio from the water are magnificent.

Cycling along Flamengo beach

TOP 10 BRAZILIAN JUICES

Refreshing Camu-Camu juice

1 Camu-Camu
This Amazonian fruit grows by seasonally flooded rivers and has a very high vitamin C content.

2 Cupuaçu
This pod-like fruit is related to cocoa and has a sweet and pungent juice. The taste is unusual but can be strangely addictive.

3 Açaí
This purple Amazonian palm berry drink has been consumed here for thousands of years. The "superfruit" is packed with vitamins.

4 Taperebá
A refreshing Amazonian fruit juice high in vitamin C. It is also supposed to have antibiotic properties.

5 Acerola
Also known as West Indian cherry juice, this is a refreshing and thirst-quenching choice.

6 Graviola
A sweet juice made from a relative of the custard apple, the soursop.

7 Caju
The juice of the Amazonian cashew-nut fruit, which is also famous the world over for its nuts.

8 Jabuticaba
A tart, berry-like fruit produces a juice popular in the state of Minas Gerais. The fruit grows directly on tree trunks.

9 Umbu
A sweet fruit juice that comes from a pulpy berry. It is particularly popular in the state of Bahia, where it grows.

10 Seriguela
This refreshing, vitamin-packed juice comes from Brazil's woodland savannah, the *cerrado*.

🔟 Outdoor Activities

Kite surfers on Praia do Pepê

1 Kite Surfing

Forte KiteSurf: MAP C2; Praia do Foguete, Cabo Frio; (22) 98113 3640; adm

The waves and strong winds to the east of Rio city, beyond Niterói, make this one of the top places for kite surfing. Surfers are attached to kites and dragged through the waves. The best place to learn the sport is in Cabo Frio town, which is 93 miles (148 km) east of Rio de Janeiro. Forte KiteSurf is a great school for kite surfing lessons.

2 Hang-Gliding and Paragliding

Just Fly: adm; www.justflyinrio. blogspot.com

Flights launch from the Pedra Bonita *(see p14)* and land at São Conrado beach *(see p99)*. Several companies, such as Just Fly, offer flights.

3 Surfing

Rico Surf: MAP B6; Posto 4, Barra da Tijuca; (21) 98777 7775; adm; ricosurf.globo.com

The best beaches for surfing are in Ipanema and Leblon – especially at Arpoador beach *(see p40)*. Boards can be rented through a school, such as Rico Surf.

4 Running

Jogging in the early morning or late afternoon is a favorite *Carioca* pastime. Top running areas include Copacabana, Ipanema, and Leblon.

5 Windsurfing

Freewind: MAP C2; Av Carlos Ermelindo Marins, Niterói; (21) 98894 3458; adm; freewindsurf.com.br

Windsurfing is excellent to the east of Rio, where lagoons and high winds make conditions ideal. Try Freewind.

6 Beach Volleyball

IBV: MAP B6; Posto 1, Praia da Barra; (21) 99158 2023; adm

A number of beaches across the city are popular spots to play this

Enjoying a game of beach volleyball

game. IBV offers beach volleyball classes on Barra and Flamengo beaches daily.

Hiking
RioXtreme: adm; rioxtreme.com

One of the best hikes is to the summit of the Pedra da Gávea *(see p14)*, and to Pico da Tijuca in the Tijuca National Park. Try RioXtreme for tours.

Rock Climbing
Climbinrio: adm; www.climb inrio.com

Sugar Loaf and Morro da Urca *(see pp16–17)* top the list of the best rock climbing spots. Other great locations include Parque Nacional do Itatiaia and the Serra dos Órgãos *(see p47)*. Climbinrio offers climbing services.

Gávea Golf and Country Club

Golf
Gávea Golf and Country Club: MAP D6; Estrada da Gávea 800, São Conrado; (21) 3323 6050; adm; www. gaveagolfclub.com.br

The best golf course in Rio is in Gávea. The 18-hole club is private, but games can be booked through concierges at the better Rio hotels.

Diving
MAP C2

Intensive factory fishing in the 1980s has damaged some of the marine life. There are still some dive sites at Arraial do Cabo, near Cabo Frio *(see p47)*, but extra care should be taken around the soft corals, sponges, and marine life.

TOP 10 OLYMPIC VENUES

Samba school parade, Sambódromo

1 Sambódromo
Rio's Carnaval parade *(see p39)* ground hosted archery and the start and finish of the marathon events.

2 Deodoro Olympic Park
This partially-restored Olympic venue hosts canoeing events. The pool here is open to local residents on weekends.

3 Maracanã
The world-famous football stadium hosted both the opening and closing ceremonies, and football finals.

4 Olympic Golf Course
Golf was an Olympic event in 2016 for the first time in 112 years; Barra Golf Club was the venue.

5 Arena Carioca
This triple stadium was the main Olympic gymnastics base in 2016, it is now a home court for Rio's main basketball teams.

6 Maria Lenk Aquatics Center
The main venue for swimming events in the 2007 Pan American Games and the 2016 Olympics.

7 Rio Olympic Park
The main Olympic venue in 2016, where the Cidade do Rock arena hosts annual music festival, Rock in Rio.

8 Lagoa Rodrigo de Freitas
Rowing and other aquatic events were held on this scenic lagoon.

9 Marina da Glória
Rio's marina was given a substantial makeover to host the Olympic sailing events.

10 Copacabana
Rio's most famous beach was spruced up for the Olympic volleyball and aquatic events that were held here.

TOP 10 Soccer

Estádio do Maracanã hosts matches between Rio's major soccer clubs

1 Estádio do Maracanã

Once the world's largest soccer stadium, the Maracanã *(see p39)* is where Pelé scored his 1,000th goal in 1969. The atmosphere at the stadium during a game is electric.

2 Flamengo

One of Rio's four big clubs. Its moment of glory was winning the first Brazilian World Championship in 1981. Famous past players include Gérson, Júnior, and Zico.

Flamengo playing Botafogo

3 Botafogo

This club's ex-players make up a roster of some of the greatest names in Brazilian soccer. Its golden era was in the 1950s and 60s when it provided most of the players for Brazil's victorious World Cup team.

4 Fluminense

Soccer was introduced to Rio de Janeiro by Englishman Oscar Cox, who went on to found Fluminense on July 21, 1902. The club remains one of Rio's most traditional, and many of its supporters are wealthy *Cariocas*. It has an intense rivalry with Flamengo.

5 Vasco da Gama

Named for the Portuguese explorer Vasco da Gama, this club is traditionally supported by Portuguese *Cariocas*.

6 The Rio-vs-São Paulo Tournament

The *Torneio Rio–São Paulo* was a tournament played between teams from the rival states Rio de Janeiro and São Paulo, and was one of the most bitterly contested tournaments. Although it's no longer held, the rivalries still stand.

7 The Rio de Janeiro State Championship

The *Campeonato Carioca*, a competition for the state's soccer clubs, was established in 1906. Fluminense and Flamengo, with more than 30 titles each, have more victories than any other club.

8 The "Maracanaço Tragedy"

"O Maracanaço" refers to the Brazilian soccer "tragedy" during the 1950 World Cup, when Brazil lost to Uruguay. The word has passed into common parlance in Brazil and is used to refer to other soccer defeats and even political debacles.

Late-afternoon beach soccer

9 Beach Soccer
www.fifa.com

Many of Rio's greatest stars learned to play soccer on makeshift pitches on the city's beaches. The players preserved such a love of beach soccer that it is now a FIFA-recognized sport in its own right.

10 Footvolley

This sport began on the beaches of Rio. Its rules are similar to volleyball, but only the feet and head can be used. Brazil remains the leading footvolley team, but is hotly pursued by some Asian nations.

TOP 10 FAMOUS CARIOCA SOCCER STARS

Superstar Leônidas da Silva

1 Leônidas da Silva (1913–2004)
Before Leônidas da Silva, Brazilian soccer was a white, middle-class game.

2 Nilton Santos (1925–2013)
A key defender in three World Cups and scorer of one of the most spectacular goals of all time in a match against Austria in 1958.

3 Didi (1929–2001)
A legendary midfielder named player of the tournament at the 1958 World Cup in Sweden.

4 Garrincha (1933–83)
Pelé's contemporary and officially the best Brazilian player other than Pelé himself, according to FIFA.

5 Gérson (b 1941)
One of the best passers in the history of soccer, who masterminded the 1970 World Cup victory.

6 Carlos Alberto (1944–2016)
Captain of Brazil's World Cup-winning team in 1970 and a great defender.

7 Jairzinho (b 1944)
A lightning-fast winger who devastated opponents in the 1970 World Cup.

8 Zico (b 1953)
One of the greatest midfielders in the history of the beautiful game.

9 Romário (b 1966)
The only player other than Pelé to score 1,000 goals in professional soccer.

10 Ronaldo (b 1976)
Nicknamed "The Phenomenon" in Brazil, he won the FIFA Player of the Year award in 1996, 1997, and 2002.

🔟 Off the Beaten Path

Exhibits in the Museu Casa do Pontal

1 Museu Casa do Pontal

This museum *(see p97)* has a charming collection of ceramic and wooden folk art from all over Brazil. Tiny figurines portray traditional daily life in enchanting tableaux.

2 Parque Ecológico Chico Mendes

This nature reserve *(see p98)* offers a taste of tropical wilderness on the doorstep of the city: sandy trails lead through mangroves, marshland and cacti groves; home to endangered caiman, turtles, birds, and butterflies. A few blocks inland from Recreio beach lies the Taxas lagoon, beside which is a lookout tower, picnic site and children's playground.

3 Ilha Grande
MAP A2

Two hours west of Rio, along the Costa Verde, is this offshore tropical paradise. Secluded beaches fringe its shores and jungle trails lead to crystalline waterfalls and lagoons. Boats visit on day cruises, or hop on a ferry from Angra dos Reis port.

4 Sítio Roberto Burle Marx

See the former home of Rio's most celebrated landscape designer, Roberto Burle Marx. His sculptures dot the lush tropical gardens here, which contain some 3,500 species of flora. The lovingly preserved house *(see p98)* contains his personal art collection. Marx's workshop and

bedroom have been kept just as he left them, giving a very personal feel to the site. Guided tours are available.

5 Pico da Tijuca
MAP D4 ■ Praça Afonso Viseu, Tijuca ■ (21) 2492 2252 ■ Open 8am–5pm daily ■ www.parquenacional datijuca.rio/amigos-do-parque/

Hike through the Tijuca National Park to the peak of Rio's tallest mountain. The ascent is steep; but your efforts will be rewarded with sublime views. The hike generally starts from 2pm.

Fortaleza de Santa Cruz, Niterói

6 Niterói
MAP C5

This city across the bay may lack its neighbor's natural wonders, but it does have great views of Rio's coastline. The 16th-century Fortaleza de Santa Cruz (Sant Cruz Fort) offers the best vantage point.

7 Valença, Vale do Café
MAP B2 ■ Valença ■ www. institutopreservale.com.br

One of the loveliest old towns in the Vale do Café, deep in Rio state. This used to be at the heart of the

Brazilian coffee empire; its colonial *fazendas* now welcome visitors with tours of the plantations and luxurious accommodation.

8 Museu do Bonde
MAP W3 ▪ Rua Lélio Gama, Centro ▪ (21) 2332 8422 ▪ Open 8am–4pm daily

Dedicated to Santa Teresa's tram system, this museum is housed in the downtown Carioca tram station. The small, but charming collection includes guards' uniforms, old photographs, model trains, ticket machines, and assorted memorabilia.

9 Feira de São Cristóvão
MAP E1/F1 ▪ Campo de São Cristóvão, Centro ▪ (21) 4108 9248 ▪ Open 10am–6pm Tue–Thu (until 4am Fri & Sat, to 8pm Sun) ▪ www.feiradesaocristovao.org.br

Always buzzing, this market (see p53) in a working-class, downtown neighborhood specializes in all things from northeastern Brazil. Stalls are packed with crafts, food, and music, with live bands performing non-stop Friday morning through Sunday evening.

10 Praia Vermelha
MAP J4 ▪ Praia Vermelha, Urca

This sheltered beach (see p74) at the foot of Pão de Açúcar is a family favorite for its calm waters and soft red sand. Nearby are local *por kilo* buffet restaurants, and the Pista Claudio Coutinho walkway (see p73).

The serene, secluded Praia Vermelha

TOP 10 RIO STATE ATTRACTIONS

Museu Imperial, Petrópolis

1 Petrópolis
MAP B2 ▪ www.museuimperial.museus.gov.br
The royal family's summer palace is now home to the Museu Imperial.

2 Búzios
MAP B2 ▪ www.buziosonline.com.br
This upscale resort town has beaches backed by restaurants and boutiques.

3 Serra dos Órgãos
MAP B2 ▪ www.riohiking.com.br
Mountain range northeast of Rio, offering great climbing and trekking.

4 Conservatória
MAP B2
A charming town tucked away in Rio's historic Coffee Valley. It is famous for its serenading street musicians.

5 Teresópolis
MAP B2
This mountain town comes alive on weekends with a bustling artisan fair in the main square.

6 Parque Nacional do Itatiaia
MAP A2 ▪ www.parquedoitatiaia.tur.br
Brazil's oldest national park offers superb bird-watching and hiking trails.

7 Região dos Lagos
MAP C2
Picturesque coastal region fringed with white, sandy beaches and salt lakes.

8 Cabo Frio
MAP C2
Cariocas come to this popular weekend escape for the beaches, surfing, snorkeling, and scuba diving.

9 Paraty
MAP A3
This beautiful colonial gold-rush town is a UNESCO World Heritage Site.

10 Mata Atlântica
MAP B2
Brazil's Atlantic coastal rain forest is home to abundant wildlife.

🔟 Activities for Children

Baixo Bebê children's play area on Leblon beach

1 Baixo Bebê
MAP L6 ■ Leblon beach

This little playground, tucked under the looming Os Dios Irmãos hill at the far end of Leblon beach, has climbing frames and sandpits *(see pp32–3)*. Kids can cool off with coconut water available at juice stalls nearby. There are child-friendly cafés and restaurants too, in one of Leblon's safest areas.

2 Parque Nacional da Tijuca

This sprawling forest park *(see pp14–15)* wrapping around Rio contains the city's highest peaks as well as dozens of trails and lookout points, making it an ideal location for a day's hiking and wildlife spotting. It is home to a rich array of wildlife, including monkeys, birds, and butterflies. There are plenty of spots around the park where families can enjoy a picnic in the shade.

3 Sugar Loaf Mountain

The views from the Sugar Loaf and Morro da Urca *(see pp16–17)* may be spectacular, but children will particularly relish the dramatic cable-car rides to the hilltops. The trails on the hills are also worth exploring. Look out for the indigenous tufted-eared marmosets. The Sugar Loaf has a café-bar and Morro da Urca has cafés and restaurants, as well as a theater that hosts popular shows and concerts for all ages.

4 Parque da Catacumba

This lushly forested, hilly park *(see p77)* overlooking Lagoa has a zip-wire adventure trail from raised platforms suspended in the trees. There are different levels suitable for adults and children – all are great fun. Entrance to the park is free, but there is a small charge for the zip-wire trail.

5 Parque das Ruínas
MAP V5 ■ Rua Murtinho Nobre 169, Santa Teresa ■ (21) 2215 0621 ■ Open 9am–4pm Thu–Sun

Containing ruins of a colonial mansion, this park offers excellent views of the city. There is a gazebo and a small playground for kids to enjoy. It also holds special programs for children over the weekends, with traditional *Carioca* music performances, plays, and exhibitions.

Nijinsky by Mazeredo, Parque da Catacumba

6 Planetário

With engaging, state-of-the-art displays, this planetarium (see p79) is one of the best in South America. As well as astronomical shows (narrated in Portuguese), it has an interesting museum that features touch displays. Kids of all ages can use the powerful telescopes to view planets and galaxies once a week.

7 BioParque do Rio

MAP E1 ■ Quinta da Boa Vista, São Cristóvão ■ (21) 3900 6672 ■ Open 9am–5pm daily ■ Adm ■ www.bioparquedorio.com.br

In addition to housing more than 1,000 animals, including large carnivores in recently enlarged open spaces, this smart, modern zoo runs an important captive-breeding program for marmosets and tamarins – the world's smallest monkeys.

8 Museu do Pontal

Founded by Belgian artist Jaques van de Beuque, this delightful folk-art museum (see p97) curates ceramic and wooden figurines from around Brazil. Intricate tableaux portray daily life, from classrooms to carnaval parades. The collection has been recognized by UNESCO as a unique anthropological record of Brazilian cultural life.

Figurines in Museu do Pontal

9 Jardim Botânico

This tropical garden behind the Lagoa Rodrigo de Freitas, with its ponds, little streams, and waterfalls, is a lovely place to while away a sunny afternoon (see pp24–5). Children will be delighted to spot monkeys and *agoutis* – rabbit-sized rodents that look like tiny deer. Café Botânico sells ice cream.

Sagui monkey, Jardim Botânico

10 Lagoa Rodrigo de Freitas

MAP F5 ■ Parque dos Patins, Av Borges de Medeiros, Lago ■ (21) 2541 7522 ■ Open daily

Rio's lagoon, between Ipanema and Jardim Botânico, has a plethora of family-friendly attractions, including swan-shaped pedaloes for hire, and the Parque dos Patins, with a skate park, bungee jumping, and trampolines. There's also a cycling track and numerous cafés dotted around its perimeter.

🔟 Bars and Nightclubs

4 Venga!
MAP K5 ▪ Rua Dias Ferreira 113-B, Leblon ▪ (21) 2512 9826 ▪ venga.com.br

One of Rio's first Spanish tapas bars, this cozy, busy little place serves small, tasty delicacies, including fresh seafood and vegetarian options which can be paired with sangria by the jug or glass, and chilled wine and beer.

5 Rio Scenarium
Lapa's plushest *samba* venue hosts live acts downstairs that play hits like *Aquarela do Brasil*, while the club upstairs plays contemporary Brazilian dance music. There is plenty of quieter sitting space in the gallery areas (see p86), which are decorated with antiques.

1 Academia da Cachaça
MAP L5 ▪ Rua Conde de Bernadotte 26G, Leblon ▪ (21) 2529 2680 ▪ academiadacachaca.com.br

This streetside bar has one of the best selections of Brazil's national drink in the city. *Cachaça* is distilled from sugarcane and is the basis of *caipirinha* cocktails.

2 Empório
MAP N5 ▪ Rua Maria Quitéria 37, Ipanema ▪ (21) 3813 2526

Popular among locals and visitors alike, this bar has live music on weekends and DJs nightly. The dance floor often shifts to the streets where people gather on sidewalks. It doesn't get lively until midnight.

3 Bip Bip
MAP G6 ▪ Rua Alm. Gonçalves 50, Copacabana ▪ (21) 2267 9696

This low-key bar down a quiet sidestreet attracts some of Rio's best musicians, who play impromptu *forro*, *pagode*, and *samba* jam sessions to devoted local fans. It's the perfect spot to enjoy an intimate and laidback Carioca night out.

Live *samba* at Rio Scenarium

Crowds dance to the live music at Carioca da Gema

6 Carioca da Gema

Arguably Rio's best live *samba* club, Carioca da Gema (*see p86*) is housed in a converted town house in Lapa, a short stroll from Rio Scenarium. Some of the best old *samba* and *choro* acts in the city play here. It is a very popular venue and gets crowded on weekends, so go early to ensure you get a table or bar space.

7 Coordenadas

MAP R1 ■ Rua da Passagem 19, Botafogo ■ www.coordenadasbar.com.br

Known for organizing wild, itinerant parties around the city for years, the Coordenadas group is now based in Botafogo. The club is spread over two floors and features multiple bars, plus a kitchen that serves up artisan burgers. Old-school rock, *música popular brasileira* (or MPB), and kara-oke liven up the dance floor here.

8 Bar Bukowski

MAP R2 ■ Rua Álvaro Ramos 270, Botafogo ■ barbukowski.com.br

Set in an old mansion in residential Botafogo, this buzzing rock bar hosts live acts on Friday and Saturday evenings. It has four bars, three dance floors, pool tables, shisha pipes, and a spacious beer garden where you can chill and listen to music all night long.

9 Quiosque Rainbow

MAP H5 ■ Av. Atlântica, 1702, Copacabana ■ (21) 7832 0126

This beachside bar opposite the Copacabana Palace Hotel serves excellent cocktails and *petiscos* (snacks) and is one of the most popular meeting spots for Rio's LGBTQ+ community.

Diners at Quiosque Rainbow

10 Armazém São Thiago

One of Rio's classic *boteco* bars (*see p86*), this local favorite in arty Santa Teresa is a great spot for a relaxing evening over a *cerveja bem geladinha* (chilled beer). Take your pick of the many *cachaças* served here. The dining menu is also a big draw, with snacks includ-ing sweet potato and *bolinhas* (gorgonzola croquettes).

TOP 10 Restaurants

4 Quadrifoglio

Situated inside the giant Barra shopping mall (see p100), this gem of a restaurant (see p101) offers a choice of indoor and outdoor terrace seating, and is one of the best options in town for Italian dining. The set lunches here include classic pasta and pizza favorites, while the evening tasting menu features more innovative, adventurous dishes, such as deliciously fresh seafood, lemon risotto and sweet apple ravioli.

1 Sud, O Pássaro Verde

This informal café (see p81) serving top-notch street food with a gastro makeover is run by feted Brazilian chef Roberta Sudbrack. With only 12 tables, no wine list and no reservations, Sud is usually busy, serving locally sourced organic produce that shines in Sudbrack's food, such as in her signature dish, okra caviar.

2 Miam Miam

For a taste of contemporary Mediterranean cuisine, head to this fine restaurant (see p75) located in an old family home in residential Botafogo. Chef Roberta Ciasca prepares a range of innovative dishes with an unexpected fusion of ingredients, such as pork with tangerine, shitake mushrooms and ginger.

3 Chez Claude

Following the closure of his award-winning restaurant Olympe, nouvelle cuisine maestro Claude Troisgros opened this superb bistro (see p95) on a Leblon residential backstreet. The French and Brazilian fusion cuisine features sharing dishes, such as eggs and caviar clarisse. The vibe is casual and tables are arranged around the open-plan kitchen.

5 Confeitaria Colombo

Featuring an Art Nouveau skylight, gilt-framed mirrors, and decorative lamps, this 19th-century coffee and pastry house (see p68) serves up all manner of treats. The feijoada (see p110) lunch on Saturdays is often accompanied by live music. The white-jacketed waiters here contribute to its traditional air of gentility.

The delightful Confeitaria Colombo

6 Lasai

Set in a beautifully restored colonial townhouse, Lasai (see p75) is another one of Rio's Michelin-starred restaurants. It is famous for its dazzling contemporary cuisine, prepared by the expert, Basque-trained chef Rafa Costa e Silva.

Private and exclusive seats at the "chef's table" in Lasai

His ten-course tasting menu creates culinary magic with vegetables and meat sourced straight from local farmers, ranchers, and fishmongers. Do not miss out on the cocktails served at the rooftop bar.

7 Esplanada Grill
Brazil is famous the world over for its grilled meat restaurants, or *churrascarias*, and none is better than the Esplanada Grill *(see p95)* – an elegant Ipanema offering. It is a popular place for business men and women who appreciate the high-quality ingredients large portions. The restaurant is also noted for its respectable wine list, which features local classics as well as organic and incense wines.

8 Benkei Asiatico
With more Japanese residents than any country in the world outside of Japan, Brazil is replete with fine Japanese restaurants. Part of a chain, Benkei Asiatico *(see p101)* serves some of the best Japanese and Indian cuisine in Rio in a buffet *rodízio* (all-you-can-eat) casual restaurant.

9 Gero Rio
Rogério Fasano's sophisticated establishment *(see p95)* is one of Rio de Janeiro's finest Italian restaurants and is located in one of its most exclusive hotels. Gero Rio specializes in delicious, fresh seafood and offers striking views over the Atlantic Ocean.

10 Espírito Santa
Santa Teresa is full of funky little restaurants and bars, and this is one of the best. Amazonian and Bahian cooking – including exquisite river fish like *pacu* – is served in an informal restaurant-bar and on a small, candle-lit roof terrace, with wonderful views of the city at night. The bartender serves some of Rio's best *caipirinhas* and the club downstairs *(see p86)* opens for dancing on Friday nights.

Informal dining at Espírito Santa

TOP 10 Shopping

Artwork for sale, Feira Hippie Market

1 Arts and Crafts from the Feira Hippie Market

There is overpriced bric-a-brac in this well-known market (see p94) in central Ipanema, but also the occasional gem. Look for models of Rocinha houses made of wood or papier-mâché and for rope sculptures made by a *favela* artist.

2 Arts, Crafts and Food from Feira de São Cristóvão

A hub of exuberant activity, this outdoor market (see p47) is worth exploring for the wide array of arts and handicrafts on offer, including jewelry, pottery and Afro-Brazilian carvings. The aromatic food stalls here sell coconut-based sweets, hot sauces and famously succulent seafood from the north-eastern region of Brazil.

3 Perfume from O Boticário

MAP W3 ■ Rua Visconde de Piraja 371, Ipanema ■ (21) 99005 4072 ■ www.oboticario.com.br

O Boticário is a Brazilian chain of cosmetic and body-care shops, similar to The Body Shop, found all over the city. It has a range of superior natural products including tasteful perfumes and aftershaves, many of which are made from scents derived from Brazilian plants.

4 Bikinis from Lenny Niemayer

MAP N5 ■ Rua Visconde de Pirajá 351 Loja 114/115, Ipanema ■ (21) 2523 3796 ■ lennyniemeyer.com

The only place in Rio that has a dress code is the beach. Brazilian swimwear is widely regarded as the most fashionable in the world – at least by models and fashionistas – and the best place to find the most trendy cuts and patterns is in the heart of Ipanema, at Lenny Niemayer. There are many other stores nearby, including Salinas and Blue Man.

5 Books from Livraria da Travessa

Part of a chain, the charming Livraria da Travessa (see p94) began life in 1975 as a tiny bookstore that quickly grew into a destination for intellectual debate, artists engaged

Cozy interior of Livraria da Travessa

in counterculture and political resistance, and "marginal" poets. Today, this literary institution offers a wide selection of Brazilian and international books, music DVDs, and great coffee.

⑥ Jewelry from Antônio Bernardo

MAP M5 ■ Shopping Leblon mall, 3rd floor, shop 302E, Av Afrânio de Melo Franco 290, Leblon ■ (21) 2523 3192 ■ www.antoniobernardo.com.br

Brazil's most stylish and exclusive jeweler has branches worldwide, but the best choice is still to be found in Brazil where it all began. A pair of earrings can set you back $6,000.

⑦ Indigenous crafts from Loja Artíndia

MAP Q1 ■ Museu do Índio, Rua das Palmeiras 55, Botafogo ■ Closed for renovation until 2025 ■ www. museudoindio.gov.br/visitas/na-loja

This shop, attached to the Museu do Índio (see p72), is the best place in town to buy crafts made by Brazil's Indigenous peoples, be it basketware, ceramics or jewelry.

⑧ Crafts from Pé de Boi

MAP W6 ■ Rua Ipiranga 55, Laranjeiras ■ (21) 2285 4395 ■ Open 9am–7pm Mon–Fri, 9am– 1pm Sat ■ www.pedeboi.com.br

This ethically conscious shop sells handicrafts sourced from artisans across Brazil, with a huge range of beautiful handmade products, from painted ceramics to woven baskets and naive-style artworks.

⑨ Babados de Folia

MAP V3 ■ Rua Regente Feijó, 57, Centro ■ (21) 2224 84095

Those wanting to take a bit of Carnaval color home or dress up during Carnaval week should head to this vibrant store in Centro. It sells everything from feather boas to sequin bikinis at reasonable prices.

⑩ Crafts from Parceria Carioca

MAP E5 ■ Rua Jardim Botânico 728 ■ (21) 2259 1437

This great shop sells fun and funky accessories and crafts made by local cooperatives in some of Rio's poorest neighborhoods. The proceeds help to fund artisan workshops.

Parceria Carioca storefront

⏸ **Rio de Janeiro for Free**

Glorious sunset over Ipanema beach

1 Sunset over Ipanema
Join the locals on Ipanema beach *(see pp32–3)* at the end of every day, when they gather to watch the sun setting over Dois Irmãos, applauding and toasting as darkness falls.

2 Museums
Centro Cultural Banco do Brasil: Rua Primeiro de Março 66, Centro; open 9am–9pm Wed–Mon (until 8pm Sun); (21) 3808 2020; culturabancodo brasil.com.br/portal/rio-de-janeiro
Many of Rio's museums are free on Sunday, and some are always free, including the Centro Cultural Banco do Brasil, Oi Futuro *(see p74)*, and the Paço Imperial *(see p29)*.

3 Free Guided Walks
Free Walker Tours: open Mon–Sat (no booking required); www.freewalkertours.com
Take a guided walk led by locals with expert knowledge of *Carioca* culture and history. Free Walker Tours are available in English and Portuguese, and cover Downtown, Copacabana, Ipanema, Lapa, the docks, Olympic Boulevard, plus evening pub crawls.

4 Capoeira
This dizzying martial art was developed in northeastern Brazil hundreds of years ago by enslaved people from Africa. You can enjoy free *capoeira* displays in the city's open spaces, such as the Feira do Rio Antigo *(see p85)* on the first Saturday of the month at 10:30am.

5 Escadaria Selarón
The colorful steps *(see p84)* leading from Lapa to Santa Teresa were the work of eccentric Chilean artist Jorge Selarón (1947–2013). He spent the last 20 years of his life creating this tribute to the area.

Colorful Escadaria Selarón

6 Parks and Gardens
Rio is a gloriously green city. As well as the jungle backdrop that is the free Parque Nacional da Tijuca *(see p14–15)*, there are many free parks and gardens, including Parque do Flamengo *(see p74)*, Parque Lage *(see p78)*, and Parque Ecológico Chico Mendes *(see p98)*.

7 Beach Activities
Rio's magnificent beaches are huge free playgrounds. You can flex your muscles at the workout

stations, watch – or dare to join – a football or volleyball game, and see displays of sand sculptures.

8 Music

Pedra do Sal: Largo João da Baiana, Rua Argemiro Bulcao, Saúde; open from 8pm Mon & Fri; mapade cultura.rj.gov.br/manchete/roda-de-samba-da-pedra-do-sal

Cariocas live and breathe to a musical rhythm. There are free concerts all weekend at the Feira de São Cristovão *(see p47)* and free samba on Monday and Friday nights in Pedra do Sal, a tiny square in Saúde.

9 City Views

Soak up stunning panoramas of Rio and its environs from its many hilltop *mirantes* (lookouts). Check out Tijuca National Park *(see pp14–15)*; Parque das Ruínas *(see p48)*; Parque da Catacumba *(see p77)*, overlooking Lagoa; and Morro da Urca *(see pp16–17)*, reached via a (steep) trail off the Pista Claudio Coutinho.

10 Churches

Most of Rio's churches are free to enter. There are some spectacular architectural wonders, including Mosteiro de São Bento *(see pp18–19)*, Igreja Santo Antônio, and Catedral Metropolitana *(see p66)*.

Inside the Catedral Metropolitana

TOP 10 BUDGET TIPS

Copacabana metro station

1 MetrôRio
Buy a MetrôRio pre-paid card to save time on queuing. It has no expiry date.

2 Cheap eats
Prato feito set meals are an affordable lunch option. *Por kilo* buffet restaurants are also reasonable and found all over the city *(see p110)*.

3 Flight savings
Some Brazilian airlines, such as LATAM and GOL, offer cheap flights online if booked in advance.

4 Cheap accommodation
Save up to 30 percent on your room rate if you book in advance online.

5 Laundrettes *(lavanderias)*
These are much cheaper than the services offered by hotels.

6 Cheap phone calls
Discount international phone cards *(cartões telefonicas internacionais)* are available from airports, bus stations, and hotels. Wi-Fi is also widely available.

7 Off-season savings
Traveling to Brazil outside the popular tourist season (April, May, August, and September) can save as much as 50 percent on the cost of your flight.

8 Apartment rental
If you are staying in Rio for more than a week, consider renting an apartment. These can be far cheaper than hotels, especially in the beach neighborhoods.

9 Hostels
Hostels offer private rooms as well as dormitory-style accommodation. These are usually – though not always – cheaper than most budget hotels.

10 Ticket agencies
Buy tickets for events from online ticket agencies *(www.ticketsforfun.com.br)*, saving time and hassle.

🔟 Carnaval Parades and Balls

A colorful float at the Sambódromo during Carnaval

① Sunday and Monday at the Sambódromo
MAP T4 ▪ **Centro** ▪ **Adm**
On the first Sunday and Monday of Carnaval, the top *samba* schools march through the Sambódromo (see p39) in *blocos* (parades) to compete for the title of champion.

② Banda de Ipanema
MAP P5 ▪ **Praça General Osório**
This is one of Carnaval's largest and most colorful street parades. Glamorous drag queens and outrageously dressed partygoers dance *samba* with tourists, families, and passersby.

③ Baile do Copa
MAP R3 ▪ **Copacabana** ▪ **Adm**
Another Carnaval tradition is the formal black-tie "Magic Ball," which is held at the Copacabana Palace hotel (see p112) on the first Saturday of Carnaval. Book tickets online (www.rio-carnival.net) or through the hotel in advance.

④ Blocos in Santa Teresa
MAP U5 ▪ **Santa Teresa** ▪ **Adm**
The highlights of this lively street party are its atmosphere and music. It takes place on a stretch between Largo dos Guimarães and Largo das Neves in Santa Teresa, and is popular with a young crowd.

⑤ Champions' Parade
MAP T4 ▪ **Centro** ▪ **(21) 4042 0213** ▪ **Adm**
The winners of the spectacular Sambódromo parades dance again on the final Saturday of Carnaval. It is easier to get tickets for this event.

⑥ Bloco Cacique de Ramos
MAP V4–W3 ▪ **Centro** ▪ **(21) 3880 9248** ▪ **Adm**
The Bloco Cacique de Ramos parade has marched through downtown Rio since 1961; today it passes by Avenida Chile. A new *samba* song is written and sung every year by one of Rio's famed *sambistas*.

⑦ Bloco de Segunda
MAP Q1 ▪ **Botafogo**
Held on the first Monday of Carnaval week, this *bloco* features dancers in elaborate costumes, including *Baianas* (Afro-Brazilian women from Bahia) in enormous flowing dresses who spin as they *samba* along Rua Marques.

8 Saymos do Egyto

MAP F6 ▪ Monte Libano, Av Borges de Medeiros 701, Lagoa ▪ (21) 2512 8833

A hit with a younger LGBTQ+ crowd dressed as pharaohs and Cleopatras, this is one of the more recent *blocos* on the scene. Viemos do Egypto was originally a nightclub party that migrated to the streets for Carnaval. The *bloco* is found at the Clube Monte Libano on Carnaval Tuesday.

9 Baile Vermelho e Preto do Flamengo

MAP G2 ▪ Sambódromo, Rua da Marquês de Sapucaí Centro ▪ (21) 2976 7310 ▪ Adm

Vermelho (red) and *preto* (black) are the colors of one of Rio's most popular soccer teams, Flamengo *(see p44)*, and are a compulsory part of the dress code at their annual ball which is held in the Sambadrome during the intervals between the Carnaval parades on the first Friday and Saturday.

10 Gala Gay at Rio Scala

MAP H2 ▪ Av Treze de Maio 23, Cinelândia ▪ (21) 2511 4140

One of Rio's most famous and lavish indoor Carnaval balls takes place at the enormous Rio Scala each year on Carnaval Tuesday. The star-studded event is televised globally and tickets are incredibly hard to secure.

Carnaval float decorations

TOP 10 SAMBA SCHOOLS

Beija Flor de Nilópolis *samba* **school**

1 Beija Flor de Nilópolis
www.beija-flor.com.br
Flying a blue and white flag, this is the most successful school since 1985, with 11 wins in all.

2 Mangueira
www.mangueira.com br/site
This popular school has won 20 times. Its colors are pink and green.

3 Império Serrano
www.sambadoimperioserrano.blogspot.com
Parading under a green flag, Serrano has had nine victories.

4 Unidos da Tijuca
www.unidosdatijuca.com.br
Winner of multiple gold standards, Tijuca's colors are yellow and blue.

5 Unidos do Viradouro
www.unidosdoviradouro.com.br
The famous Carnaval queen Juliana Paes danced for this school. Red and white are its colors.

6 Salgueiro
www.salgueiro.com.br
A top school with nine victories, colored red and white.

7 Estácio de Sá
www.gresestaciodesa.com.br
One-time victors in 1992, its colors are red and white.

8 Imperatriz Leopoldinense
www.imperatrizleopoldinense.com.br
A successful school with eight victories, its colors are green, yellow, and white.

9 Portela
www.gresportela.org.br
This school has won the Sambódromo *samba* contest 22 times under a blue and white flag.

10 Vila Isabel
www.unidosdevilaisabel.com.br
With six victories to date, this club flies the white and light blue flag.

TOP 10 Festivals and Shows

Indigenous people performing at Parque Lage on Dia do Indio

1 Festa de São Sebastião
Jan 20

The patron saint of Rio is honored with a series of processions that leave from the church of São Sebastião dos Capuchinhos in Tijuca and make their way to the city center.

2 Carnaval
Feb/Mar ▪ Sambódromo: MAP T4; Rua Marquês de Sapucaí, Centro; (21) 2976 7310; adm

Carnaval takes place at the start of Lent. The parades take place in Oscar Niemeyer's Sambódromo stadium *(see p39)*.

3 Dia do Indio
Apr 19

This celebration commemorates the first Inter-American Indigenous Congress, which took place in Michoacán, Mexico in 1940. Indigenous people from all over Brazil participate.

4 Festas Juninas
Jun

These extensive religious festivals are held throughout June in homage to St. Anthony and St. John. Locals dress up in checked shirts, drink spiced cocktails, feast on traditional food, and dance to lively *forró* music.

5 Anima Mundi – Festival Internacional de Cinema de Animação
Jul ▪ animamundi.com.br

One of the world's premier celebrations of animation showcasing work from mainstream, independent, and avant-garde film-makers from all over the world. Every year, after the festival takes place in Rio, it moves on south to São Paulo.

6 Festa Literária Internacional de Paraty
Jul/Aug ▪ www.flip.org.br

This gathering of international writers takes place in the colonial port town of Paraty, which is located

Samba Schools Parade at Carnaval

three hours south of Rio de Janeiro. It offers live music and other events. Past guests have included novelists such as Toni Morrison, Salman Rushdie, and Michael Ondaatje.

7 Festival Internacional de Cinema do Rio

Sep–Oct ■ www.festivaldorio.com.br
One of South America's largest and most diverse film festivals, this two-week event showcases independent films from all over the world, with a focus on Latin America. Full features and shorts are shown in cinemas throughout the city.

8 The Festa de Nossa Senhora da Penha

MAP D3 ■ Largo da Penha 19, Penha ■ (21) 3219 6262 ■ Oct ■ www. basilicasantuariopenhario.org.br
Catholic pilgrims crawl or walk on their knees up the steps to this church for the city's most traditional festival.

Presente de Yemanjá celebration

9 Yemanjá Day
Dec 31

This New Year's Eve celebration is dedicated to Yemanjá the Orixá, the Goddess of the Sea. Devotees dressed in white gather on beaches from midnight until dawn to worship her and toss offerings in the Atlantic.

10 New Year's Eve
Dec 31

Rio's biggest celebration is not Carnaval but Reveillon, or New Year's Eve. Millions of people gather on Copacabana beach *(see p30–31)* for the party which features free concerts and spectacular fireworks displays *(see pp30–31)*.

TOP 10 LIVE ACTS IN RIO

Jorge Ben Jor at a performance

1 Jorge Ben Jor
The founding father of the funky Rio sound still plays live shows in Rio.

2 Iza
The former cover artist and now ground-breaking Latin Grammy award winner wows the crowds at the biennial Rock in Rio festival.

3 Orquestra Imperial
Made up of popular local musicians, this dance-hall *samba,* or *gafieira*, band is a Carnaval party stalwart.

4 Chico Buarque
The political conscience of his generation, Buarque sometimes performs gigs in Lapa and at Viva Rio in Flamengo.

5 Marisa Monte
A trained classical musician, Monte has become one of Rio de Janeiro's biggest international stars.

6 Sandra de Sá
The queen of Rio *samba* soul is famous for her covers of classic Motown tracks and is another festival regular.

7 Martinho da Vila
Writer of many of the official Carnaval parade *sambas* for the Unidos de Vila Isabel *samba* school.

8 Zeca Pagodinho
The king of Rio party music plays an infectious variant of *samba* called *pagode*.

9 Seu Jorge
One of Brazil's biggest music and movie stars who made his name at the Circo Voador *(see p86)* club in Lapa.

10 Nação Zumbi
This inventive *mangue bit* band attracts a huge following with its sell-out Rock in Rio concerts.

Top 10 Rio de Janeiro Area by Area

Cable car carrying visitors to the top of Sugar Loaf Mountain

Centro	**64**
The Guanabara Bay Beach Neighborhoods	**70**
Lagoa, Gávea, and Jardim Botânico	**76**
Santa Teresa and Lapa	**82**
Copacabana, Ipanema, and Leblon	**90**
Western Beaches	**96**

🔟 Centro

Rio's bustling city center sits on a promontory that juts out into Guanabara Bay. A wave of rash construction in the early 20th century led to many of the area's finest buildings being razed to the ground, and the center lost much of the architectural unity. However, reminders of Rio's grand past can still be found around Centro's broad avenues, where modern buildings are interspersed with delightful palaces and Baroque churches, as well as fascinating museums and art galleries.

Detail, Igreja Santo Antônio

CENTRO

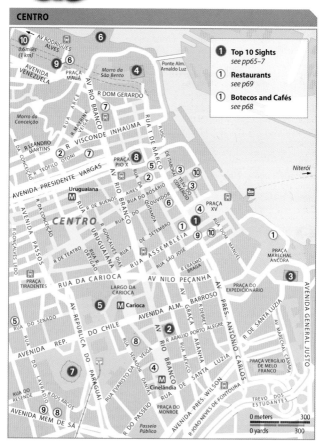

1 Top 10 Sights
see pp65–7

1 Restaurants
see p69

1 Botecos and Cafés
see p68

Interior of Igreja de Nossa Senhora do Monte do Carmo, Praça XV

1 Praça XV

Dominated by the Paço Imperial, this flagstone square (see pp28–9) near the ferry port preserves the memory of Rio under Portuguese rule. Until the Proclamation of the Republic in 1889, this square was the political center of Rio and Minas Gerais, and after the arrival of the royal family, it was the seat of power for Brazil. Praça XV is home to many historic buildings, restaurants, shops, as well as two of central Rio's finest churches – Igreja de Nossa Senhora do Monte do Carmo and Igreja da Ordem Terceira de Nossa Senhora Carmo da Antiga Sé.

2 Museu Nacional de Belas Artes

Rio's foremost art gallery houses one of Latin America's most impressive collections (see pp20–21). Vitor Meirelles' apology for colonialism, *A Primeira Missa no Brasil*, is displayed here. More interesting Modernist Brazilian work is represented by painters such as Cândido Portinari, Emiliano Di Cavalcanti, and the *antropofagista* Tarsila do Amaral, who defined the modern Brazilian style.

3 Museu Histórico Nacional

Devoted entirely to the history of Brazil, Museu Histórico Nacional is one of the largest museums in the country (see pp26–7). Panels and displays trace the development of Brazil from the Stone Age, when the first inhabitants left paintings in the Serra da Capivara, up until the first days of the republic. A café next to the lobby serves delicious coffee, fresh juices, and snacks. Visit during the week or early in the morning to avoid the crowds.

4 Mosteiro de São Bento

Rio's oldest church (see pp18–19) is also one of Brazil's most beautiful. Its modest facade belies a lavish interior of Baroque carvings, including an opulent, gilded Blessed Sacrament Chapel. On Sundays at 10am, you can hear the Benedictine monks, who live in the adjacent monastery, singing a Latin mass.

Facade of Mosteiro de São Bento

Catedral Metropolitana de São Sebastião

BOTECOS

The restaurants and bars that dot the city from Ipanema to the center are called *botecos* or *botequins*. All are busy with waiters rushing around carrying glasses of beer and snacks. Two of the most popular *botecos* in the center are Labuta Bar *(see p68)* and Garota de Ipanema *(see p92)*, where *bossa nova* was popularized in the early 1960s.

⑤ Igreja Santo Antônio
MAP W3 ■ **Largo da Carioca s/n** ■ **(21) 2262 0129** ■ **Open 9am–6pm Mon–Fri (until noon Sun)**

Rio's second-oldest convent is set in a series of colonial churches on a hill overlooking Largo da Carioca. The bright interior is decorated with tiles and statues of St. Anthony. Women are often seen praying to the saint, who is said to be a provider of husbands.

⑥ Museu do Amanhã
MAP H1 ■ **Praça Mauá 1, Centro** ■ **(21) 3812 1812** ■ **Open 10am–6pm Tue–Sun** ■ **Adm** ■ **museudoamanha.org.br**

Perched on a promontory jutting out into the bay, this exciting museum is dedicated to science, particularly focusing on humanity's place in the cosmos and our role in the evolution of planet Earth. It is very popular, and there are long queues on weekends. Tickets for August and September must be booked online in advance.

⑦ Catedral Metropolitana de São Sebastião
MAP W4 ■ **Av República do Chile 245** ■ **(21) 2240 2669** ■ **Open 7am–5pm daily (museum: 9am–4pm Wed (until noon Sat & Sun)** ■ **www. catedral.com.br**

Resembling a Maya pyramid in architectural style, the impressive Modernist Catedral Metropolitana was designed by architect Edgar de Oliveira da Fonseca between 1976 and 1984. The cathedral's basement houses a Sacred Art Museum that preserves age-old artifacts of the Portuguese royal family.

⑧ Candelária Church
MAP W2 ■ **Praca Pio X** ■ **(21) 2233 2324** ■ **Open 7:30am–3:30pm Mon–Fri, 9am–noon Sat, 9am–1pm Sun**

This grand Italianate temple has long been the church of choice for

Interior of Candelária Church

high-society Rio. Built between 1775 and 1894, the church was modeled on Lisbon's Basílica da Estrela; the marble for the interior was shipped from Verona. The Candelária gets its name from a chapel built in homage to Our Lady of Candles, which stood on the same site from 1610.

9 Museu de Arte do Rio (MAR)

MAP H1 ▪ Praça Mauá 5, Centro ▪ (21) 3031 2741 ▪ Open 10am–5pm Thu–Sun ▪ Adm ▪ museude artedorio.org.br

This iconic structure, designed by Brazilian architect Alfonso Eduardo Reidy, houses the art of Rio. It was once a police station and a bus station, both of which are now united under the museum's distinctive wavy roof. The artworks here depict Rio's dynamic history, with sculptures, paintings, and images from colonial times to the modern day.

Exhibit at Museu de Arte do Rio (MAR)

10 Porto Maravilha

Porto Maravilha, Gamboa ▪ www.portomaravilha.com.br

A multi-billion Real makeover of Rio's docks transformed the downtown district into a gleaming new hub. The docks feature Eduardo Kobra's huge Etnias mural and the impressive AquaRio, the largest aquarium in South America with more than 350 different species of marine animals.

A DAY IN THE HISTORIC CENTER

▶ MORNING

Begin with a visit to a temporary exhibition in the **Paço Imperial** *(see p29)* or the fine churches that cluster around nearby **Praça XV** *(see pp28–9)*. There is often some interesting bric-a-brac in the little market on the square and the shop inside the **Paço Imperial** is great for browsing. Walk north across the square under the **Arcos de Teles** archway and along the charming **Travessa do Comércio** *(see p29)*. Cross Rua 1 de Marco to visit the grand **Candelária Church** then head back to Rua Ouvidor. The streets off Ouvidor throng with activity and give a real feel of Rio's working life. Next, take a left onto Rua Gonçalves Dias and have lunch at the **Confeitaria Colombo** at No. 32 *(see p68)*.

AFTERNOON

To get to the regenerated docks area, head north across Avenida Presidente Vargas and up Rua Acre past the picturesque **Morro da Conceição** neighborhood to the **Museu de Arte do Rio**. Get a combined ticket for that and the **Museu de Amanhã** (advance booking recommended), and when you have had your fill of images of Rio, walk across to the **Praça Maua**. From there, take a stroll along Avenida Rodrigues Alves to check out the brightly rejuvenated docks area, including Eduardo Kobra's huge **Etnias mural**, before heading back down to the **Beco das Sardinhas** *(see p68)* for a cold *chopp* beer and some freshly fried sardines.

See map on p64

Botecos and Cafés

① Café Curto
MAP X3 ■ Rua da Assembléia 10 ■ (21) 96948 3225 ■ Open 8am–8pm Mon–Fri

This gourmet café serves the best espresso in Rio, and what's more, you pay what you like.

② Casa Paladino
MAP W2 ■ Rua Uruguaiana 226 ■ (21) 2263 2094 ■ Open 7am–8:30pm Mon–Fri

One of Centro's most traditional *botecos* often plays live music at night. Try the prawn *petisco*.

③ Botecos on Travessa do Comércio
MAP X2

The *botecos* that line this alley by Praça XV *(see pp28–9)* are a favorite haunt for *Cariocas* in search of cold beer and tasty snacks after work.

Botecos on Travessa do Comércio

④ Amarelinho
MAP X4 ■ Praça Floriano 55B ■ (21) 3549 8434 ■ Open 11am–1am daily

This bright yellow *boteco* has been around since the early 20th century.

⑤ Labuta Bar
MAP V3 ■ Av Gomes Freire 256 ■ (21) 3148 2156 ■ Open 7–9am & 11am–7pm Mon–Fri, 11:30am–7pm Sat

Cariocas and city workers pack out this tiny bar, famous for its delicious *petiscos* and ace cocktails.

The buzzing Confeitaria Colombo

⑥ Confeitaria Colombo
MAP W2 ■ Rua Gonçalves Dias 32 ■ (21) 2505 1500 ■ Open 11am–6pm Mon–Fri (from 10am Sat) ■ www.confeitariacolombo.com.br

This Portuguese coffee shop *(see p52)* serves snacks as well as cakes.

⑦ Botecos on Beco das Sardinhas
MAP W2 ■ Rua Miguel Couto

Sample beers and snacks from the *botecos* along this bustling street.

⑧ Boteco Belmonte
MAP W4 ■ Av Mem de Sá 82 ■ (21) 2507 0971 ■ Open 11:30am–1am daily

A lively bar popular with Lapa's young arty crowd. Try the *chopp* draft beer with some tasty *petiscos* (tapas).

⑨ Bar Brasil
MAP W4 ■ Av Mem de Sá 90 ■ (21) 2509 5943 ■ Open 10am–11:30pm Tue–Sat (until 4:30pm Sun)

This German *boteco* offers a range of Bavarian food and beer.

⑩ Rio Minho
MAP W2 ■ Rua do Ouvidor 10 ■ (21) 2509 2338 ■ Open 11am–5pm Mon–Fri

Excellent seafood is served in this longstanding *boteco*, opened in 1884. Popular at lunchtime.

Restaurants

1 Albamar
MAP X2 ■ Praça Marechal Âncora ■ (21) 2240 8428 ■ Open 11:30am–5pm Mon–Fri (until 6pm Sat & Sun) ■ $$$

Once under threat of demolition in 1933, this tower restaurant, known for delicious seafood, was so popular with Rio's high society that it survived.

2 Verde Vicio
MAP X2 ■ Rua Buenos Aires 22 ■ (21) 2233 9602 ■ Open 11am–3:30pm Mon–Sat ■ $

Low-priced healthy eating options are served canteen-style in an airy space.

3 Cais do Oriente
MAP X2 ■ Rua Visconde de Itaboraí 8 ■ (21) 2233 2531 ■ Opening times vary, call ahead ■ $$$

Enjoy Brazilian versions of Asian and Mediterranean dishes. There is live *samba* and *choro* on weekends.

4 Bistro do Paço
MAP X2 ■ Paço Imperial, Praça XV ■ (21) 2262 3613 ■ Open 11am–5pm Mon–Fri (from noon Sat) ■ $

Choose from a menu of light lunches at this pleasant bistro.

Simple interior of Bistro do Paço

PRICE CATEGORIES
For a three-course meal for one with half a bottle of wine, taxes, and extra charges. Prices quoted in US dollars.

$ under $25 $$ $25–$50 $$$ over $50

---

5 Low Fire
MAP X2 ■ Rua da Alfândega 7 ■ (21) 2283 4095 ■ $

This lively, casual restaurant dishes up great Brazilian steaks and burgers American barbecue-style.

6 Costela do Beco
MAP X2 ■ Beco dos Barbeiros 12 ■ (21) 96775 6563 ■ Open 11am–4pm Mon–Fri ■ $$

Tucked down a side street, with simple decor, this place specializes in superb Brazilian steaks and ribs.

7 Mosteiro
MAP W1 ■ Rua São Bento 13/15 ■ (21) 2233 6478 ■ Open noon–4pm Mon–Fri ■ $$$

Named for the nearby Mosteiro de São Bento *(see pp18–19)*, this place is famous for its *bacalhau* (salt cod).

8 Al-Kuwait
MAP X4 ■ Av Treze de Maio 23 ■ (21) 2240 1114 ■ Open 9am–7pm Mon–Fri ■ $$

The menu at this Arabic and North African restaurant also includes some Brazilian fare.

9 Mangue Seco
MAP V3 ■ Rua do Lavradio 23 ■ (21) 3852 1947 ■ Open 11am–1am daily (until 3pm Mon, Tue) ■ $$

By night this is mostly a bar serving fine *cachaças*, but by day it's a restaurant serving Brazilian dishes.

10 Hachiko
MAP X3 ■ Travessa do Paço 10 ■ (21) 3819 3293 ■ Open 11:30am–4pm & 6–11pm Mon–Fri (until 11pm Sat) ■ $$$

Savor Brazilian–Japanese fusion food. There's great sashimi and yakisoba.

See map on p64

🔟 The Guanabara Bay Beach Neighborhoods

War Memorial in Glória

The history of fashionable Rio can be traced through a series of beach neighborhoods that line Guanabara Bay. In colonial times, the aristocracy frequented Centro, then Glória, with its yacht-filled harbor, and, in the mid-20th century, Flamengo and Botafogo. When the water became polluted, they headed for Copacabana. Today, Ipanema and Leblon are the places to be, but the bay neighborhoods retain stately buildings, attractive parks, and interesting little museums and galleries.

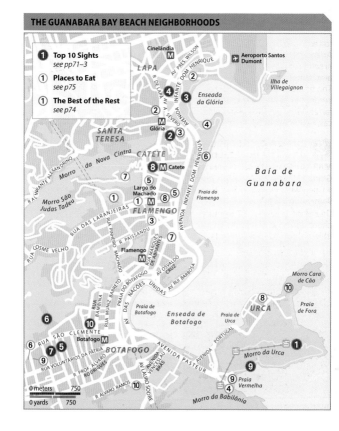

THE GUANABARA BAY BEACH NEIGHBORHOODS

1 **Top 10 Sights**
see pp71–3

1 **Places to Eat**
see p75

1 **The Best of the Rest**
see p74

Sugar Loaf Mountain and Morro da Urca, with Botafogo in the foreground

1 Sugar Loaf Mountain

This famous peak *(see pp16–17)* sits in Guanabara Bay, and stares out toward Niterói and the inky-blue Atlantic. The view from the top is as breathtaking as from Cristo Redentor and looks best in the early morning. The first European reached the summit in 1817. Nowadays, it is far easier to get there – by cable car, helicopter, or hiking trail.

2 Igreja Nossa Senhora da Glória do Outeiro

MAP X6 ▪ Praça Nossa Senhora da Glória 135, Glória ▪ (21) 2225 2869 ▪ Open 9am–noon & 1–5pm Mon–Fri 9am–noon Sat & Sun

One of the prettiest 18th-century churches in Rio is perched on a little hill surrounded by woods,

Interior of the church

and overlooks the bay. The polygonal interior, lined with fine painted blue and white *azulejo* tiles, is impressive. The church was the favorite of the Brazilian royal family. Emperor Dom Pedro II *(see p37)* was baptized here.

3 Monumento Nacional aos Mortos da II Guerra Mundial (War Memorial)

MAP X5 ▪ Av Infante Dom Henrique 75, Glória ▪ (21) 2240 1283 ▪ Open 10am–4pm Tue–Sun

This beautifully balanced plinth supports two concrete columns topped by a convex slab, and is one of Rio's most impressive Modernist monuments. It was designed by architects Marcos Konder Neto and Hélio Ribas Marinho in 1960 to commemorate the Brazilian soldiers who were killed in fighting in Italy during World War II.

4 Praça Paris

MAP X5 ▪ Av Augusto Severo, Glória

Located between Glória, Lapa, and Centro, this leafy square is an ideal place to take a leisurely walk among fountains and statues. It was designed by Alfredo Agache, taking inspiration from the French gardens of the early 20th century. Be careful while using cameras and smartphones as muggings happen in this area.

Brazilian composer Heitor Villa-Lobos

5 Museu Villa-Lobos

MAP Q1 ■ Rua Sorocaba 200, Botafogo ■ (21) 2226 9818 ■ Open 11am–5pm Tue–Fri ■ museuvillalobos.museus.gov.br

Heitor Villa-Lobos is Latin America's most respected classical composer. Between 1917 and his death in 1959, he produced over 1,000 original works influenced by both foreign composers and Brazilian musical styles, particularly *choro*. His best-known piece is the *Bachianas Brasileiras*. The museum, set in the musician's former home, displays his personal effects such as his musical instruments, manuscripts, and recordings. It also hosts performances of his music.

6 Santa Marta Favela

MAP G4 ■ Above Rua São Clemente ■ (21) 99177 9459 ■ favela santamartatour.blogspot.com

An elevator takes visitors up to this generally peaceful *favela* with brightly colored houses and great views from the hillside of Botafogo. It is the location for Spike Lee's 1995 music video for Michael Jackson's *They Don't Care About Us*, and a statue of Jackson has been erected there in recognition. Favela Santa Marta Tours offer guided tours by local residents.

7 Museu do Índio

MAP Q1 ■ Rua das Palmeiras 55, Botafogo ■ (21) 3214 8700 ■ Open Apr: 9am–5:30pm Tue–Fri, 1–5pm Sat, Sun & hols ■ www.museudoindio.gov.br

When the Europeans arrived, Brazil was inhabited by more than 5 million Indigenous people divided into at least 1,000 groups. Much of their culture was wiped out with the onset of slavery. The museum is temporarily closed for refurbishment. On reopening, it will display a number of Indigenous objects, with rooms devoted to information panels and slide shows, a *Guaraní maloca* (communal thatch house), a gift shop, and a library.

8 Museu de Folclore Edison Carneiro

MAP H3 ■ Rua do Catete 179–181, Catete ■ (21) 3826 4327 ■ Open 10am–6pm Tue–Fri, 3–6pm Sat & Sun ■ cnfcp.gov.br

Established in 1968, the Museum of Folklore displays arts and crafts from all over Brazil. The comprehensive museum features carved

Colorful painted houses in Santa Marta Favela

models and tableaus of rodeos, circuses, and festival scenes, which, when switched on, work like music boxes. Over 17,000 exhibits and bibliographic documents with audiovisual displays, and hundreds of ceramic objects and photographs, paint a vivid picture of Brazil's cultural life.

Museu de Folclore Edison Carneiro

9 Pista Cláudio Coutinho
MAP J4 ■ Open 6am–6pm daily

This walking track snakes its way around the base of the Sugar Loaf and Morro da Urca, with a side trail leading up to the top of Morro da Urca. The views are wonderful throughout. The bayside path cuts through woodland filled with tiny, buffy tufted-eared marmosets and brilliantly colored tanagers, and dips onto the Praia de Fora beach. Walks are coolest in the early morning, and the trail is one of the safest in urban Rio because of the huge army presence in Urca.

10 Casa de Rui Barbosa
MAP Q1 ■ Rua São Clemente 134, Botafogo ■ (21) 3289 4600 ■ Open 10am–6pm Tue–Fri (until 8pm last Tue of month), 2–6pm Sat–Sun & hols ■ Adm ■ www.casaruibarbosa.gov.br

Rui Barbosa was one of the most influential politicians in the early years of the Brazilian republic. His former home, one of many stately 19th-century town houses to have been preserved in Botafogo, is now a museum. There are often free classical music concerts in the main hall and the gardens are an oasis of peace and quiet away from the bustle of busy Botafogo.

A CLIMB UP MORRO DA URCA AND THE SUGAR LOAF MOUNTAIN

The sides of the twin boulder mountains of **Morro da Urca** and the **Sugar Loaf Mountain** (see pp16–17) appear to be impossibly steep. But there is an easy path leading to the summit of Urca and a more challenging trail winding up the Sugar Loaf Mountain. The trail at the foot of Urca is called the **Pista Cláudio Coutinho**. This is guarded by a small gateway that is opened at around 6am every morning. Look for the signpost at the eastern end of **Praia Vermelha** in Urca. The flat, paved path winds around the base of the **Sugar Loaf Mountain**, right next to the deep indigo water of Guanabara Bay. After about 330 yards (300 m), a signpost points left off the main path, up the steep mountainside to the top of Urca. Before long, it becomes possible to see right across Guanabara Bay to the city center. The summit of Urca takes about an hour to reach from the start.

Be sure to bring plenty of water, a camera, sun protection, and a hat. Cool off beneath the trees or in one of the cafés at the top of Morro da Urca. The path up the Sugar Loaf Mountain is more difficult to access, and some stretches must be climbed. It is possible to climb the mountain with a tour company like Rio Hiking (www.riohiking.com.br). It usually takes around two hours to reach the summit, but the unforgettable vistas of Copacabana, Ipanema, Corcovado and Tijuca are worth every bit of effort. In case you are uncertain about climbing up all the way, you can opt for the cable car which offers an easy access to the summit.

See map on p70 ←

The Best of the Rest

1 Parque Guinle
MAP G3/H3 ■ Rua Gago
Coutinho 66, Laranjeiras
■ Open 24hrs daily

This peaceful little park is a popular picnic spot for local families, with a play-ground and duck pond. Overlooking the park is Palacio Laranjeiras the original owner's stately residence.

2 Chafariz da Glória
MAP X2 ■ Rua de
Glória 122

Built in 1772, this is one of the city's oldest public drinking fountains. It has been restored several times over the years.

3 Memorial Getúlio Vargas
MAP X6 ■ Praça Luís de
Camões, Glória ■ (21) 2245 7577
■ Basement museum: open 10am–
7pm Tue–Sun

Brazil's authoritarian president lived in Rio for almost 30 years. These 50-ft (15-m) tall tapering marble columns sitting in an algae-filled pond commemorate him.

Boats moored in Marina da Glória

4 Marina da Glória
MAP X6 ■ Glória

Boats leave from this harbor for tours around Guanabara Bay. Cruises usually take about four hours.

5 Castelinho do Flamengo
MAP H3 ■ Praia do Flamengo
158, Flamengo ■ (21) 2205
0655 ■ Open 10am–8pm Tue–
Sat (until 6pm Sun)

This whimsical Art Nouveau building is home to a concert hall and arts center.

Castelinho do Flamengo

6 Parque do Flamengo
MAP H3 ■ Flamengo

Roberto Burle Marx landscaped these extensive gardens. There are wonderful views of the Sugar Loaf Mountain.

7 Casa de Arte e Cultura Julieta de Serpa
MAP H3 ■ Praia do Flamengo
340, Flamengo ■ (21) 2551 1278
■ Open 9am–6pm Mon (until
11:30pm Tue–Sat), 4–7pm Sun
■ https://julietadeserpa.com.br

This Art Nouveau building houses a series of restaurants, bars, and exhibition spaces.

8 Oi Futuro Flamengo
MAP H3 ■ Rua Dois de
Dezembro 63, Flamengo ■ (21) 3131
3060 ■ Open 11am–8pm Tue–Sun
■ www.oifuturo.org.br/cultura/
oi-futuro-flamengo

Exhibitions at this ambitious cultural center combine the diverse fields of art, science, and technology, with hands-on displays.

9 Praia Vermelha
MAP J4 ■ Urca

A pretty, secluded beach with soft pink sand and gentle waves.

10 Fortaleza de São João
MAP J4 ■ Av João Luís Alves,
Urca ■ Open 9am–4pm Mon–Fri ■ Adm

Estacio de Sá (see p59) founded this fort in 1565. Only a Baroque gate of the original structure remains.

Places to Eat

PRICE CATEGORIES

For a three-course meal for one with half a bottle of wine, taxes, and extra charges. Prices quoted in US dollars.

$ under $25 $$ $25–$50 $$$ over $50

1 Rotisseria Sírio Libaneza
MAP H3 ▪ Largo do Machado 29 ▪ (21) 2146 4915 ▪ Open 8:30am–9pm Mon–Sat ▪ $

Tuck into Middle Eastern dishes and tropical fruit smoothies at this spot.

2 Laguiole Lab
MAP X4 ▪ Av Infante Dom Henrique 85 ▪ (21) 2517 3129 ▪ Open noon–5pm Mon–Fri ▪ $$

Contemporary cuisine is the specialty at this formal restaurant in the Museu de Arte Moderna *(see p39)*.

3 Café Lamas
MAP H3 ▪ Rua Marques de Abrantes 18, Flamengo ▪ (21) 2556 0799 ▪ Open 10am–2am daily ▪ $$

This café has been serving steak, seafood, and daily specials since 1874.

4 Círculo Militar
MAP J4 ▪ Praca General Tibúrcio, Urca ▪ (21) 2295 3397 ▪ Open 6am–10pm Mon–Fri, 8am–10pm Sat & Sun ▪ $$

A good-value *por kilo* venue *(see p110)* set at the foot of Pão de Açúcar, overlooking Praia Vermelha.

5 Adega Portugália
MAP H3 ▪ Largo do Machado 66a, Catete ▪ (21) 2558 2821 ▪ Open 8am–1am Mon–Sat (until 11pm Sun) ▪ $$

Try the roast goat casserole or the kasseler pork at this open-fronted venue on Largo do Machado.

6 Lasai
MAP P1 ▪ Largo dos Leões, 35 ▪ (21) 3449 1834 ▪ Open 7:30–10pm Tue–Sat ▪ $$$

One of Rio's best offerings, Lasai features artisically presented dishes.

7 The Maze
MAP H3 ▪ Rua Tavares Bastos 414, Casa 66, Catete ▪ (21) 2558 5547 ▪ Open 1–5pm Wed–Sun ▪ $

The best Indian food in Rio can be found here. There's a curry buffet on offer for Sunday lunch, plus a Friday night jazz club once a month.

8 Bar Urca
MAP J4 ▪ Rua Cândido Gaffrée 205, Urca ▪ (21) 2295 8744 ▪ Open 8:30am–10:30pm Mon–Fri, 9:30am–9pm Sat & Sun ▪ $$

A fine Urca institution known for its Portuguese-style seafood dinner.

Interiors of Bar Urca

9 Reduto
MAP G4 ▪ Rua Conde de Irajá 90, Botafogo ▪ (21) 99164 3324 ▪ Open 7pm–1am Thu–Sat ▪ $$

Set in a colonial mansion with a leafy beer garden, Reduto serves adventurous contemporary cuisine. There is live music on weekends.

10 Miam Miam
MAP R1 ▪ Rua General Góes Monteiro 34, Botafogo ▪ (21) 9836 64420 ▪ Open noon–11:30pm Tue–Sat (until 5pm Sun) ▪ $$

Enjoy flavorful Mediterranean food in this atmospheric restaurant-bar.

See map on p70

🔟 Lagoa, Gávea, and Jardim Botânico

These prosperous, upper-middle-class neighborhoods lie around Lagoa Rodrigo de Freitas, between Ipanema and Leblon, and Corcovado. They are the evening haunts of Rio's rich and fashionable, and the numerous clubs, bars, and restaurants that pepper the streets are always busy. Nightlife is at its wildest in Gávea, where the *botecos* around Praça Santos Dumont are particularly lively toward the weekends. During the day, shady parks and tropical gardens tempt visitors away from the beach.

Orchid, Jardim Botânico

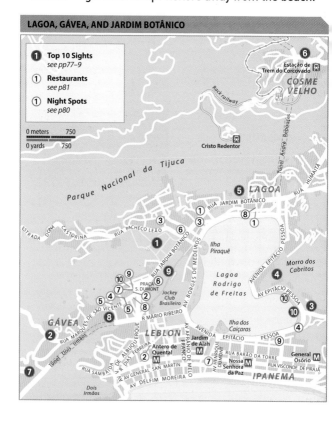

LAGOA, GÁVEA, AND JARDIM BOTÂNICO

1 **Top 10 Sights**
see pp77–9

1 **Restaurants**
see p81

1 **Night Spots**
see p80

0 meters   750
0 yards   750

Mural at the Instituto Moreira Salles

1 Jardim Botânico

There are 140 ha (348 acres) of broad, palm-tree-lined avenues, shady paths, and lawns dotted with classical fountains in these beautiful botanical gardens *(see pp24–5)*. Many of the trees here – like the *pau brasil*, for which the country was named – are threatened with extinction in the wild. Their branches and fruits and the tropical flowers that fill the garden attract birds and animals from the nearby Floresta da Tijuca. Allow at least three hours for a visit and come at the beginning of the day or after 3pm, when the temperatures are cooler.

Palm-lined walkway, Jardim Botânico

2 Instituto Moreira Salles

MAP D6 ■ Rua Marquês de São Vicente 476, Gávea ■ (21) 3284 7400 ■ Open noon–6pm Tue–Fri (from 10am Sat & Sun) ■ ims.com.br

This attractive 19th-century house is set in lush grounds landscaped by renowned architect Roberto Burle Marx. The colorful murals on the patio are the work of the famous Brazilian painter Cândido Portinari *(see p21)*. The building is now an exhibition space and café.

3 Fundação Eva Klabin

MAP F6 ■ Av Epitácio Pessoa 2480, Lagoa ■ (21) 3202 8550 ■ Open for tours (times vary, check website) ■ Adm (free on weekends and public hols) ■ www.evaklabin.org.br

A fascinating collection containing 2,000 works of art spanning four millennia – from ancient Egyptian sculptures to Impressionist land-scapes. The museum is housed in the early 20th-century former home of Klabin, whose possessions and furniture are also displayed. Tour guides accompany all visitors.

4 Parque da Catacumba

MAP N4 ■ Av Epitácio Pessoa 3,000 ■ (21) 4105 0079 ■ Open 9:30am–4:30pm Tue–Sun (Dec–mid-Mar: until 5:30pm Tue–Sun) ■ lagoaaventuras.com.br

Sculptures by Brazilian artists such as Bruno Giorgi and Alfredo Ceschiatti dot this woodland near the Lagoa. A lookout point here offers great views.

Corcovado looming over Parque Lage

5 Parque Lage
**MAP M2 ■ Rua Jardim Botânico
414, Jardim Botânico ■ (21) 3257
1800 ■ Open 9am–5pm daily**

An imposing, early-20th-century
mansion, housing the School of
Visual Art and fronted by Neo-
Classical fountains, dominates
this park. The house and gardens
were designed by Englishman
John Tyndale for a wealthy *Carioca*
industrialist. The mansion's atrium
now houses an arty café. Trails lead
from the park to the summit of
Corcovado and require a guide.

6 Largo do Boticário
**MAP G3 ■ Rua Cosme Velho
822, Cosme Velho**

This lovely square takes its name from
Joaquim Luiz da Silva Souto, who was
the pharmacist (*boticário*) to the royal
family and lived here from 1831. The
enclave has colonial-style buildings
dating from the 1920s (some with
picturesque *azulejos* – Portuguese

Largo do Boticário charming facade

FAVELAS

Many *Cariocas* live in impoverished
areas with poor-quality housing and
substandard sanitation. Although most
favelas (**below**) are home to law-abiding
people, many are plagued by gang
violence. These communities have a
rich cultural heritage – *samba*, Brazilian
soccer, and Carnaval all began here.
Only ever visit *favelas* on a guided tour.

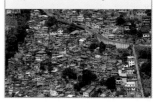

tiles), cobbled streets, and a fountain.
The square lies close to the Trem
do Corcovado funicular station in
Cosme Velho, and can be accessed
through the Rebouças tunnel. It is
worth visiting en route to the famous
statue of Cristo Redentor *(see p12)*.

7 Rocinha Favela
**MAP D6 ■ Favela Tour: www.
favelatour.com.br**

The largest *favela* in South America
takes its name from the little farm,
or *rocinha*, that once stood on its now
heavily urbanized hills, which teem
with some 100,000 people. The community here is served by its own local
shops, TV and radio stations, restaurants, and bars. Brazilian born

Marcelo Armstrong's Favela Tour offers tourists an insight into local culture and life in Rocinha.

8 Planetário

MAP K4 ■ Rua Vice-Governador Rubens Berardo 100, Gávea ■ Open 10am–5pm Tue–Sun ■ Telescopes: open 7pm Wed ■ Adm ■ www.planeta.rio

Gávea's stellar attraction (see p49), this complex features a museum of the universe, ultra-modern domes that can project thousands of stars onto their walls, and a viewing area, which offers star-gazing sessions through powerful telescopes.

9 Jockey Club Brasileiro

MAP L4 ■ Praça Santos Dumont 31, Jardim Botânico ■ (21) 3534 9000 ■ Races: 5–11pm Mon & Tue, 2–8pm Sun ■ www.jcb.com.br

Rio's course is perfect for a day at the races, or go in the evening and enjoy a meal there. The 3,000-seater grandstand dates from 1926.

10 Parque do Cantagalo

MAP P4 ■ Parque do Cantagalo, Av Epitácio Pessoa s/n, Lagoa

This circular park winds around Lagoa Rodrigo de Freitas. There is a running track situated close to the water here, as well as cafés and bars where locals come to relax in the shade. Swan-shaped pedal boats and kayaks can be hired at the lake.

The serene Parque do Cantagalo

A DAY IN RIO'S PARKS AND GARDENS

▶ MORNING

Start the day with a stroll around **Jardim Botânico** (see pp24–5). Try to arrive as close to 8am as possible and with binoculars in hand for the best chance to spot brilliantly colored birds such as tanagers, cotingas, and several hummingbirds, as well as small mammals like *paca* and *agouti*. There is a kiosk at the entrance that gives out free maps of the gardens in multiple languages, explaining where the important sights, including glasshouses such as the **Orquidarium**, are situated. At about 11am, as the morning heats up, consider taking a helicopter flight out over **Corcovado** (see pp12–13) from the helipad at Heliponto da Lagoa, just south of **Jardim Botânico**. The views of **Cristo Redentor** (see p12) from the air are amazing.

AFTERNOON

Have lunch at one of the kiosks overlooking **Lagoa Rodrigo de Freitas** on the eastern shore of the lake, which is in close proximity to the **Parque da Catacumba** (see p77). Drink plenty of juice or water and walk across Avenida Epitácio Pessoa for a 40-minute hike through the park, to the 427-ft- (130-m-) high lookout point at the **Mirante do Sacopã**. If there are no guards around, then be vigilant in the park or walk in a group. Head to **Parque Lage** by taxi for a pony ride or another light walk in the rain forest. Finish the afternoon with tea in the mansion's café.

See map on p76 ←

Night Spots

Diners at Hipódromo

1 Bar Jóia Carioca
MAP M3 ▪ Rua Jardim Botânico 594 ▪ (21) 2539 5613 ▪ Open 6am–2am daily

This unpretentious street-corner bar attracts an eclectic young crowd at weekends and in the evenings.

2 Garota da Gávea
MAP K4 ▪ Praça Santos Dumont 148 ▪ (21) 2274 2347 ▪ Open 11:30am–2am daily

On weekends, scores of people gather at this lively bar for *petiscos* (tapas) and drinks.

3 Belmonte
MAP N2 ▪ Rua Jardim Botânico 617 ▪ (21) 2239 1649 ▪ Opening times vary, call ahead

Bakeries like this one play an integral part in Brazil's nightlife, serving *empadas* (stuffed filo pies) all day.

4 Bar Rebouças
MAP N2 ▪ Rua Maria Angélica 197, Jardim Botânico ▪ (21) 2286 3212 ▪ Open 7am–1am Mon–Fri, 5pm–midnight Sat

A no-frills bar with a solid reputation for chilled beer and excellent snacks.

5 Bar Simpatia da Gávea
MAP K4 ▪ Marquês de São Vicente 68, Gávea ▪ (21) 2294 5796 ▪ Open 7am–1am daily

This friendly sports *boteco* is a great place to watch televised local soccer derbies while sipping ice-cold beer.

6 Inverso Gávea
MAP L4 ▪ Praça Santos Dumont 31 ▪ (21) 3687 9448 ▪ Opening times vary, call ahead

With an outdoor deck facing the Jockey Club, this is a lively spot to celebrate after the races

7 BG Bar
MAP K4 ▪ Praça Santos Dumont 126B, Gávea ▪ (21) 2512 0761 ▪ Open 7am–1am daily

Popular among people from the "BG" (Baixo Gávea) neighborhood, this is an ideal place to enjoy music and beers.

8 La Carioca Cevicheria
MAP N2 ▪ Rua Maria Angélica 113A, Lagoa ▪ (21) 2226 8821 ▪ Open noon–midnight Tue–Sat (until 10pm Sun), 6:30–11pm Mon

Try the *ceviche*, marinated fish, and pisco sours at this Peruvian restaurant.

9 Bar Lagoa
MAP P5 ▪ Av Epitácio Pessoa 1674 ▪ (21) 2523 1135 ▪ Open noon–midnight daily

Petiscos and cocktails are on offer at this age-old *boteco*. There's often live music on Fridays and weekends.

10 Badalado Lagoa Club
MAP N4 ▪ Av Epitacio Pessoa, Lagoa ▪ (21) 99593 2428 ▪ Open 11:30am–9pm Mon–Wed (until midnight Thu–Sun)

Munch on tasty burgers as you soak up the view in this lakeside café.

Restaurants

1 Mr Lam
MAP N2 ■ Rua Maria Angélica
21 ■ (21) 2286 6661 ■ Opening times
vary, call ahead ■ $$$

A stylish, glass-walled Chinese
restaurant with fabulous views.

2 CT Boucherie
MAP N2 ■ Rua Dias Ferreira
636 ■ (21) 2266 0838 ■ Open noon–
midnight daily ■ $$$

An excellent French bistro known
for its affordable lunch buffet.

3 La Bicyclette
MAP L3 ■ Rua Pacheco
Leão 320, shop D ■ (21) 3256 9052
■ Open 8:30am–9pm Tue–Fri (until
8pm Sat & Sun) ■ $

This French bakery offers brunches,
snacks, and hearty sandwiches.

4 Árabe da Gávea
MAP K4 ■ Rua Marquês de
São Vicente 52, Shopping da Gávea
■ (21) 3825 3000 ■ Open noon–11pm
Tue–Sun (until 10pm Mon) ■ $

One of Rio's best Arabic restaurants
bustles after dark.

5 Couve-Flor
MAP L3 ■ Rua Pacheco Leão
724 ■ (21) 3923 5315 ■ Open
11am–5pm Mon–Fri ■ $$

A lunchtime *por kilo* venue, where
you pay by the weight on your plate.

6 Sud, O Pássaro Verde
MAP E5 ■ Rua Visconde de
Carandaí 35, Jardim Botânico ■ (21)
3114 0464 ■ Open 6–10pm Tue–Sat,
noon–5pm Sun ■ $$$

Dine on street food turned haute
cuisine in Roberta Sudbrack's
latest hotspot.

7 Anna Ristorante
MAP N5 ■ Av Epitácio Pessoa
1104 ■ (21) 3813 2622 –midnight
Mon–Thu (until 1am Fri & Sat), noon–
11pm Sun ■ $$

Sublime Italian dishes and a range of
good-value wines are on offer here.

8 Bacalhau do Rei
MAP K4 ■ Rua Marquês de
São Vicente 11A ■ (21) 2239 8945
■ Open 11am–1pm Mon–Sat (until
9pm Sun) ■ $$

This family restaurant is popular with
Rio's Portuguese community.

9 Braseiro da Gávea
MAP K4 ■ Praça Santos
Dumont 116 ■ (21) 2239 7494
■ Open 11:30am–1am Sat–Wed
(until 2:30am Thu & Fri) ■ $$

Serving variations on the traditional
Brazilian meal, this restaurant is a
popular meeting point for locals.

10 Guimas
MAP K4 ■ Rua José Roberto
Macedo Soares 5 ■ (21) 2259 7996
■ Open noon–1am daily ■ $$

Carioca celebrities lunch at this
rustic restaurant, serving traditional
Portuguese and Brazilian cuisine.

Rustic ambience at Guimas

🔟 Santa Teresa and Lapa

Charming architecture, cobbled streets, and a sense of community spirit give Santa Teresa an identity of its own. This unique character coupled with the superb panoramas have made the area popular with both tourists and locals. Brilliantly colored mosaic steps connect Santa Teresa with its neighbor, Lapa, which was destitute until a renaissance began in the late 1990s. Inspired by the return of the Circo Voador club, the area was transformed into the city's hottest night spot.

Escadaria Selarón detail

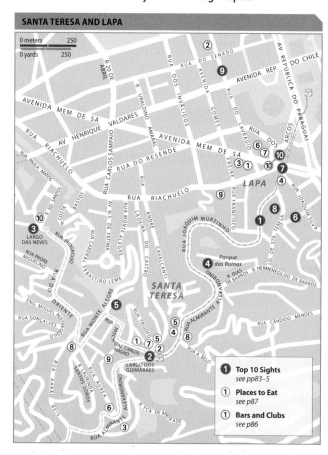

SANTA TERESA AND LAPA

0 meters 250
0 yards 250

1 **Top 10 Sights**
see pp83–5

1 **Places to Eat**
see p87

1 **Bars and Clubs**
see p86

A tram in Santa Teresa

① Tram Rides

Tram terminal: MAP V5; Rua Lélio Gama; (21) 2240 5709 ■ Trams run every 20 min, 8am–5:40pm Mon–Fri, 10am–5:40pm Sat, 11am–4:40pm Sun ■ Adm

Trams are the best way to reach Santa Teresa from Centro. Packed full of passengers, they jerk their way from Estacao Carioca next to the Catedral Metropolitana de São Sebastião (see p66), across the Arcos da Lapa, and up the steep streets of Santa Teresa. Following a temporary closure in 2011, the trams have been reinstated. They run to Dois Irmaos, with four stops en route in Santa Teresa.

② Largo dos Guimarães
MAP V6

Many of Santa Teresa's best eateries are clustered around this square,

including Espírito Santa (see p86) and Bar do Mineiro (see p87). The area also features arts and crafts shops, and nearby, on Rua do Aqueduto, is a yellow booth shaped like a tram, where the model trams found in many of Santa Teresa's restaurants are made by artisan Getúlio Damado.

③ Largo das Neves
MAP T5

The smaller of Santa Teresa's two praças (town squares) is a great place to sit and watch the world go by. There are several botecos and restaurants here serving cold beer, pizza, and seafood dishes. It is the starting point of the Santa Teresa Carnaval parade (see p58).

Parque das Ruínas

④ Chácara do Céu
MAP V5 ■ Rua Murtinho Nobre 93, Santa Teresa ■ (61) 3521 4369 ■ Open noon–5pm Wed–Mon ■ Adm (free on Wed)

The Chácara mansion, which has fantastic views over the city center, houses an exquisite museum featuring European and Asian art and antiques, as well as modern Brazilian works. Located next door is the Parque das Ruínas (see p48) – a park containing the shell of another colonial mansion.

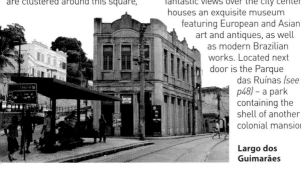

Largo dos Guimarães

The 18th-century aqueduct turned viaduct, Arcos da Lapa

5 Museu Casa Benjamin Constant

MAP U5 ■ Rua Monte Alegre 255, Santa Teresa ■ (21) 9011 1840 ■ Open 1–5pm Wed–Sun ■ Adm

This is the former home of Benjamin Constant, a political philosopher who led the republican movement and formulated key political ideas including the national motto, *Ordem e Progresso* (Order and Progress). The museum contains many personal items and offers great views.

6 Escadaria Selarón

MAP W5 ■ Rua Joaquim Silva, Lapa

These steps link Rua Joaquim Silva in Lapa with Ladeira de Santa Teresa in Santa Teresa. Their official name is the Escadaria do Convento de Santa Teresa but locals refer to them as the Escadaria Selarón – in homage to the Chilean artist, Jorge Selarón, who lived here for 30 years in a house halfway up the stairs and decorated them with colored and mirrored tiles.

The colorful Escadaria Selarón

7 Arcos da Lapa

MAP W4

Lapa is dominated by this aqueduct passing over Avenida Mem de Sá, which was built in 1724 to transport water from the Santa Teresa forest to the public drinking fountain near Largo da Carioca. Trams now run across the arches to and from Santa Teresa; lively bars and arts centers draw crowds to the adjoining square.

RONNIE BIGGS

Ronnie Biggs was a member of the gang that carried out "The Great Train Robbery" in England in 1963. He fled to Rio, settling in Santa Teresa. Biggs could not be extradited as he had fathered a Brazilian child. He returned voluntarily to the UK in 2001 because of ill health. He was arrested, but then released from prison on compassionate grounds in 2009 and died in 2013.

8 Convento de Santa Teresa

MAP W5 ■ Ladeira de Santa Teresa 52, Santa Teresa ■ (21) 2224 1040 ■ Open 9am–5pm Mon–Sat

The Santa Teresa district is named after this austere 18th-century convent which was built in honor of St. Teresa – founder of the Discalced Carmelite order of the Catholic Church and disciple and friend of St. John of the Cross. When it was completed in 1757, this became the first female convent in Brazil. Although much of the convent is closed to visitors, there is a small museum as well as access to the very spot where St. Teresa was born and the little garden where she used to play as a child.

9 Feira do Rio Antigo
MAP W4

On the first Saturday of each month, there is a lively antiques and bric-a-brac fair on Rua do Lavradio, northeast of Arcos da Lapa. The streets fill up with old-fashioned, second-hand furniture and house-hold items, as well as people dancing to live bands playing *samba* and, unusually for Rio, tango.

Feira do Rio Antigo

10 Circo Voador
MAP W4 ■ Rua dos Arcos s/n, Lapa ■ (21) 2533 0354 ■ www. circovoador.com.br

This concert arena and its coterie of musicians and artists have revitalized Lapa, which was once dangerous and decrepit. Shows at the Circo attracted visitors and brought new life to old *samba* clubs, encouraging new clubs to open. Some of Rio's best acts, including Seu Jorge, began here. The Circo is a great place to check out Rio's cutting-edge live talent.

TWO NIGHTS OF MUSIC IN LAPA

▶ FRIDAY

There is nowhere better to get acquainted with the bewildering diversity of Brazilian musical styles than in Lapa on a Friday night. Begin at around 8pm with an ice-cold *chopp* beer in **Boteco Belmonte** (see p68) on Avenida Mem de Sá (where there is a fun-filled street party on Friday and Saturday nights). *Choro*, which was popular in Rio before *samba*, can be heard live at **Carioca da Gema** (see p86), which is also on Avenida Mem da Sá. This club has a great pizza restaurant. At about 10pm, leave **Carioca da Gema** for some *gafieira* or ball-room *samba*, played by a big band fronted by a single singer. *Gafieira* is best heard some 300 ft (91 m) away at the **Clube dos Democráticos** (see p86). Be pre-pared to dance and be danced with. After this, soak up some live *samba* at the nearby **Rio Scenarium** (see p86) – the former is small and intimate while the latter is larger with a Bohemian atmosphere. Both play famous *samba* standards.

SATURDAY

If Friday has not left you exhausted, come back to this area on Saturday evening to the **Circo Voador** for more Rio funk, or dance north of **Largo da Lapa** to the tune of northeastern Brazilian *forró* played on accor-dion, triangle, and *surdo* drum. Other options include *bossa nova* electronica at **Espírito Santa** (see p86), or more from the endless list of Brazilian musical styles.

See map on p82 ←

Bars and Clubs

Live music at Carioca da Gema

1 Carioca da Gema
MAP W4 ■ Av Mem de Sá 79, Lapa ■ (21) 98556 0834 ■ Open 7pm–1:30am Mon–Fri, 9pm–1:30am Sat & Sun

One of Rio's best *samba* and *choro* bars and dance clubs. Upstairs is a Brazilian restaurant, where different live acts perform.

2 Rio Scenarium
MAP V3 ■ Rua do Lavradio 20, Lapa ■ (21) 3147 9000 ■ Open 7pm–late Tue–Fri, 8pm–late Sat

A large *samba* club featuring live bands on the ground floor, plus bars and dance floors on the upper levels.

3 Sacrilégio
MAP V4 ■ Av Mem de Sá 81, Lapa ■ (21) 3970 1461■ Open 7pm–4am Tue–Fri, 8pm–4am Sat

Excellent live acts play in this *samba* club located in an 18th-century house decorated in green and white.

4 La Esquina
MAP W4 ■ Rua Joaquim Silva 141, Lapa ■ (21) 2507 5383 ■ Open 6pm–late Tue–Sun

Always lively, this small corner bar is a great place to start the evening.

5 Espírito Santa
MAP V6 ■ Rua Almirante Alexandrino 264, Santa Teresa ■ (21) 2507 4840 ■ Open noon–midnight daily

Upstairs is a restaurant decorated with modern art and a terrace while downstairs is an atmospheric club.

6 Bar Improviso
MAP W4 ■ Ave Mem de Sá 80, Lapa ■ (21) 3852 5172 ■ Open 6pm–late Thu–Sat

This live club is the place to get on the dance floor and show off your *samba* and *pagode* moves.

7 Teatro Odisséia
MAP W4 ■ Av Mem de Sá 66, Lapa ■ (21) 2226 9691 ■ Open 11pm–midnight Fri, 24hrs Sat & Sun

A converted warehouse that rocks to the sound of live bands at weekends, and also hosts art exhibits and plays.

8 Armazém São Thiago
MAP U6 ■ Rua Áurea 26, Santa Teresa ■ (21) 2232 0822 ■ Open noon–midnight Mon–Sat (until 10pm Sun)

Also known as Bar do Gomes, this Santa Teresa bar buzzes with charm and character.

9 Clube dos Democráticos
MAP V5 ■ Rua da Riachuelo 91, Lapa ■ (21) 2252 4611 ■ Open 9pm–late Wed–Sat, 9am–5pm & 8–11:45pm Sun

This 19th-century ballroom has a huge stage and hosts ballroom *samba* and *gafieira* bands on weekends.

Samba show, Clube dos Democráticos

10 Circo Voador
The best of Rio's emerging funk acts play alongside established stars in Lapa's principal concert hall *(see p85)*. Many well-known singers got their big break here.

Places to Eat

1 Bar do Mineiro
MAP V6 ▪ Rua Paschoal Carlos Magno 99, Santa Teresa ▪ (21) 2221 9227 ▪ Open 11am–midnight daily ▪ $

Try the *bolinhos de bacalhau* (salt cod fritters) and *feijoada* (rich meat and bean stew).

2 Sobrenatural
MAP V6 ▪ Av Almirante Alexandrino 432, Santa Teresa ▪ (21) 2224 1003 ▪ Open noon–10pm Wed–Mon ▪ $$$

Terrific seafood is on offer here. There is live *samba* and *choro* on Fridays.

Outdoor dining at Aprazível

3 Aprazível
MAP U6 ▪ Rua Aprazivel 62, Santa Teresa ▪ (21) 96741 3850 ▪ Open noon–11pm Thu–Sat, 9am–6pm Sun ▪ $$$

Sample traditional dishes such as *galinhada caipira* (chicken risotto).

4 Adega do Pimenta
MAP V6 ▪ Rua Almirante Alexandrino 296, Santa Teresa ▪ (21) 2224 7554 ▪ Open noon–10pm Mon–Fri (until 8pm Sat, 6pm Sun) ▪ $$

Enjoy creative German dishes here, including *coelho assado* (roast rabbit).

5 Portella
MAP U6 ▪ Rua Páscoal Carlos Magno 139, Santa Teresa ▪ (21) 2507 5181 ▪ Open 5pm–1am Tue–Fri, noon–1am Sat, Noon–8pm Sun ▪ $

This Bohemian Paulistano-run *boteco* serves vegan and vegetarian northeastern mains.

PRICE CATEGORIES

For a three-course meal for one with half a bottle of wine, taxes, and extra charges. Prices quoted in US dollars.

$ under $25 $$ $25–$50 $$$ over $50

6 Alda Maria
MAP U6 ▪ Rua Almirante Alexandrino 1116, Santa Teresa ▪ (21) 2232 1320 ▪ Open 11am–7pm Mon–Sat, 2–7pm Sun ▪ $

This local bakery serves Portuguese cakes and pastries, including *pasteis de nata* (custard tarts). It has good coffee and a cozy atmosphere.

7 Café do Alto
MAP V6 ▪ Rua Páscoal Carlos Magno 143, Santa Teresa ▪ (21) 2507 3172 ▪ Open 9am–5pm Thu–Sun ▪ $

Belying its plain interior, this tiny bar serves superb and inexpensive northeastern cuisine.

8 Mô Café
MAP V6 ▪ Rua Santa Cristina 181, Santa Teresa ▪ (21) 2215 9037 ▪ Open 11am–7pm daily ▪ $$

This unpretentious place serves Portuguese food, and is famous for its signature *bacalhau* (salt cod) dishes.

9 Térèze
MAP U6 ▪ Rua Felício dos Santos 15, Santa Teresa ▪ (21) 3380 0220 ▪ Open 7:30–10:30am & noon–11pm daily ▪ $$$

The elegant restaurant in the Hotel Santa Teresa is pricey but top rated.

10 Goya Beira
MAP U5 ▪ Largo das Neves 13, Santa Teresa ▪ (21) 2232 5751 ▪ Open 5:30pm–midnight daily ▪ $

A busy *boteco* with a glass-fronted bar. *Cariocas* come here to enjoy the cold *chopp* (draft beer) and *petiscos* after work.

Following pages Elaborate Carnaval float in the Sambódromo

TOP10 Copacabana, Ipanema, and Leblon

Rio's association with the beach is strong, courtesy of the stunning Copacabana and Ipanema beaches, whose golden sands look south across the Atlantic. These beaches are backed by a series of bustling neighborhoods: Copacabana and Leme lie behind Copacabana beach, and Ipanema beach backs onto Arpoador, Leblon, and Ipanema. While Arpoador, Ipanema, and Leblon attract an exclusive crowd, Copacabana and Leme beaches feature people from all walks of life.

Gay Pride flags along a section of Ipanema beach

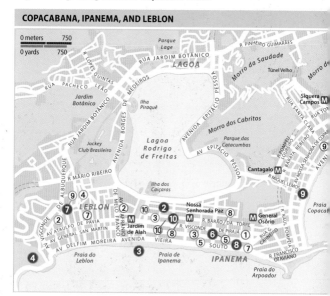

COPACABANA, IPANEMA, AND LEBLON

1 Praia de Copacabana

Rio's most famous stretch of beach (see pp30–31) is a vast 4-mile (6.4-km) sweep of powder-fine sand along the shores of the Atlantic. It is backed by a broad, four-lane avenue studded with Art Deco apartment blocks and towering hotels, the most famous being the Copacabana Palace (see p112). The avenue is lined on either side by wave-patterned mosaic pavements and has cafés and juice kiosks along its length.

2 Ipanema's Fashionable Streets

MAP M5 ■ Ipanema

Ruas Garcia d'Avila, Visconde de Pirajá, and Nascimento da Silva in Ipanema are home to some of the most exclusive designer boutiques, jewelry shops, and cafés in Rio (see pp94–5). Top Brazilian brands such as Lenny Niemayer and Antonio Bernardo (see pp54–5) vie for street space with big international names such as Louis Vuitton. Although it is possible to find bargains in shops like Toulon (see p94), prices are above average.

Ipanema and Leblon beaches

3 Ipanema and Leblon Beachlife

Ipanema and Leblon beaches are where fashion-conscious and LGBTQ+ Rio comes to lounge and relax in the sun (see pp32–3). An afternoon here is an essential experience. Bring as little as possible – sun-shades, deck chairs, snacks, and drinks are readily available on the beach.

4 Dois Irmãos

MAP K6 ■ Leblon

The "Two Brothers" – twin peaks that tower over Leblon – look particularly beautiful at dusk, when the sky turns pink and the waves are bottle-green. A lookout from Dois Irmãos offers great views over Leblon and Ipanema is reachable from the beach end of Avenida Ataúlfo de Paiva in Leblon.

Dois Irmãos tower over Leblon

Map labels:
0.6 miles (1 km)
Túnel Novo
Morro da Babilônia
deal verde
AV. PRINCESA ISABEL
LEME
ACABANA
Praia do Leme
Morro do Leme
TICA
Praia de Copacabana
Oceano Atlântico

1 **Top 10 Sights**
see pp91–3

1 **Places to Eat**
see p95

1 **Shopping**
see p94

Morro do Leme, at the northern end of Praia de Copacabana

5 Morro do Leme

This boulder hill watches over Copacabana from the Leme end of the beach *(see p31)*. It is a great spot to visit on a Sunday afternoon, when lively *samba* bands play near the sea-food kiosks. Paths and a climbing trail wind around the rock, but these are not safe without a tour guide – assaults and robberies are not uncommon here.

6 Garota de Ipanema

MAP N5 ■ Rua Vinicius de Moraes 49, Ipanema ■ (21) 2523 3787

In the early 1960s, the poet Vinícius de Moraes and his composer friend Antônio Carlos Jobim met regularly in this little bar. Inspired by a beautiful girl who used to pass by, the duo wrote the song *Garota de Ipanema*. When Brazilian guitarist João Gilberto, his wife Astrud, and US

jazz saxophonist Stan Getz recorded it in English as *The Girl from Ipanema*, they popularized *bossa nova*.

7 Rua Dias Ferreira

MAP K5

Some of the best restaurants and bars in the city line this upmarket, chic street at the end of Leblon. It is worth heading down here for an evening stroll before deciding where to dine. Restaurants range from family-run businesses, such as Celeiro *(see p95)*, to the likes of Sud, O Pássaro Verde *(see p52)* and Sushi Leblon *(see p95)*, which were founded by internationally awarded chefs. Cuisines range from French to modern Brazilian, Japanese, *churrascaria (see p110)*, and Asian-South American fusion. Dress codes are informal.

8 Casa de Cultura Laura Alvim

MAP P6 ■ Av Vieira Souto 176, Ipanema ■ (21) 2332 2016 ■ Open 1–10pm daily ■ www.casadecultura lauraalvim.rj.gov.br

Patron of the arts Laura Agostini Alvim founded this arts center in her old house in Ipanema. It exhibits artworks from Alvim's friends and admirers, including Angelo de Aquino, Paulo Roberto Leal, Roberto Moriconi, and Rubens Guerchman, and hosts visiting exhibitions, small concerts, and book launches. It also has an arts cinema and theater.

Garota de Ipanema

⑨ Museu da Imagem e da Som

**MAP Q5 ■ Av Atlântica 3432
■ www.mis.rj.gov.br**

The futuristic Museum of Image and Sound dominates Avenida Atlântica – its zigzag lines and terraces break up the ranks of tower blocks that line the avenue along Copacabana Beach. Expected to open to the public by the end of 2023, the museum is worth a visit for its impressive exterior as well as its high-tech exhibits which focus on Rio's incomparable heritage of music and dance.

Museu da Imagem e da Som

⑩ Museu H. Stern

**MAP M5 ■ Rua Garcia d'Avila 113, Ipanema ■ (21) 2259 0030
■ Open 10am–7pm Mon–Fri, 10am–4pm Sat ■ www.hstern.com.br**

The workshops in Brazil's largest upmarket jewelry chain are open to tour groups, who are encouraged to watch while stones are cut, polished, and set. Knowledgeable guides help understand the processes. Visits end at the museum shop, where carefully lit display cases show pieces from H. Stern's latest jewelry catalog.

BOSSA NOVA

Bossa nova is gentrified *samba*, sung in a spoken or whispered voice. Born in the 1950s, when Moraes, Jobim, and Gilberto began composing songs together, *bossa nova* became internationally famous with Camus' 1960 film *Black Orpheus*. It can be heard at the eclectic Rio Scenarium nightclub in Lapa *(see p86)*.

A DAY AT THE BEACH

▶ MORNING

Pack your beach bag with the minimum and bring a moderate amount of cash. To blend in with the locals, women can slip on a *tanga* (bikini) paired with a *canga* (sarong). Men can dress in board shorts over a *sunga* (rectangular-cut speedos), and wear a loose T-shirt. Finish the look with a pair of sunglasses and *chinelos* (flip-flops) – all available in shops at Ipanema and Copacabana. Put a novel and sun cream (factor 30) in your beach bag and head to one of the many juice kiosks in **Praia de Ipanema** and **Praia de Copacabana** for an *agua de coco* (coconut water) or a cup of *açai* *(see p41)*. Arrive on the beach before 9:30am to sunbathe. You will not overheat as the water here is surprisingly chilly. Swim at **Praia de Leblon**, which has the cleanest water. Areas with strong currents are always flagged.

AFTERNOON

Beachwear is acceptable everywhere except in formal lunchtime restaurants. Have a relaxed meal, a coffee, and browse in the shops along **Rua Garcia d'Avila**. From 3:30pm people begin surfing, cycling, and playing beach volleyball or soccer. Mingle with the locals or just jog along the warm sand. Romantic strolls along the waterfront are wonderful in the afternoon and beach massages are popular as the air gets cool. After sunset, head to a *boteco* like **Garota de Ipanema** in Ipanema for an ice-cold *chopp* (draft beer). Return to the hotel to change before going out to one of the many restaurants along **Rua Dias Ferreira**.

See map on pp90–91 ←

Shopping

① Feira Hippie Market
MAP P5 ▪ Praça General Osório ▪ Open 9am–6pm Sun

Praça General Osório's Sunday bric-a-brac market has stalls selling crafts, household items, and clothes.

② Shopping Leblon
MAP L5 ▪ Av Afrânio de Melo Franco 290 ▪ (21) 2430 5122

This mall on Leblon's largest shopping street houses a large number of shops of both local and international brands. It also has restaurants, a multiplex, and children's play area.

③ Blue Man
MAP F6 ▪ Rua Visconde de Pirajá 351, Shops C & D, Ipanema ▪ (21) 2247 4905

Perfect for those looking for the latest beach fashion, this designer store offers stylish bikinis and swim shorts.

④ Loja Fla
MAP H5 ▪ Av Nossa Senhora de Copacabana 219C ▪ (21) 2295 5057

Fla stocks shirts and all manner of merchandise emblazoned with the red and black of Flamengo, Rio's best known soccer team.

⑤ Bergut
MAP F6 ▪ Rua Visconde de Pirajá, 547, Ipanema ▪ (21) 3592 8008

This liquor shop and bistro has a huge cellar with some 1,800 wines and craft beers from all over Brazil and South America.

⑥ Empório Saúde
MAP F6 ▪ Shop 111, Ipanema ▪ (21) 2247 6361

This health food café and store sells a wide range of health and beauty products, as well as vegan snacks and Amazonian fruit and nuts.

⑦ Mundo Verde
MAP R3 ▪ Av Nossa Senhora de 380, Copacabana ▪ (21) 2256 8634

Find a variety of organic products at this health store, which has numerous branches in Rio. Stock up on healthy food supplements such as energy bars and veggie snacks.

⑧ Gilson Martins
MAP N5 ▪ Rua Visconde de Pirajá 462B ▪ (21) 2227 6178

This shop's range of bright, funky bags are crafted from a variety of materials, such as leather, plastic, and vinyl, and come in a variety of *Carioca* shapes – from a soccer ball to the Sugar Loaf.

Funky bags at Gilson Martins

⑨ Havaianas
MAP Q4 ▪ Av Nossa Senhora de Copacabana 691 ▪ (21) 2549 8969

Choose from myriad colors and designs at this local branch of Brazil's famous designer flip-flop chain.

⑩ Livraria da Travessa
MAP M5 ▪ Rua Visconde de Pirajá 572, Ipanema ▪ (21) 3205 9002

The best bookshop in town also stocks CDs and magazines in English, and has a delightful restaurant.

Places to Eat

1 Cipriani
MAP R3 ■ Av Atlântica 1702, Copacabana ■ (21) 2548 7070 ■ Opening times vary, call ahead ■ $$$
The Copacabana Palace's *(see p112) haute cuisine* restaurant serves north Italian fare in an opulent dining room.

2 Sushi Leblon
MAP K5 ■ Rua Dias Ferreira 256, Leblon ■ (21) 2512 7830 ■ Open noon–4pm & 6pm–1:30am Mon, noon–1:30am Tue–Sat, 1–11:30pm Sun ■ $$$
The first in the city to experiment with Japanese-Western fusion cuisine.

3 Alessandro e Frederico Café
MAP M5 ■ Rua Garcia d'Avila 134, Shop C/D, Ipanema ■ (21) 2521 0828 ■ Open 8am–1am daily ■ $$
A favorite with Ipanema's socialites, this restaurant serves tasty Italian cuisine and good-value set breakfasts.

4 Chez Claude
MAP E6 ■ Rua Conde de Bernadotte 26, Leblon ■ (212) 3579 1185 ■ Open 6:30pm–midnight Mon–Sat, noon–4pm Sun ■ $$$
Watch your dinner being prepared in the open kitchen of this fine French-Brazilian bistro *(see p52)*.

5 Zazá Bistrô Tropical
MAP N6 ■ Rua Joana Angélica 40, Ipanema ■ (21) 2247 9101 ■ Open noon–11:30pm Sun–Thu (until midnight Fri & Sat) ■ $$$
This lively bistro, serves Brazilian, Mediterranean, and Asian food.

PRICE CATEGORIES
For a three-course meal for one with half a bottle of wine, taxes, and extra charges. Prices are quoted in US dollars.
$ under $25 $$ $25–$50 $$$ over $50

6 Yaya Comidaria
MAP H3 ■ Rua Gustavo Sampaio 361, Shop A, Leme ■ (21) 3496 7754 ■ Open noon–midnight, Mon–Sat (until 9pm Sun) ■ $$
Enjoy a buffet featuring meat, fish as well as good vegetarian dishes here.

7 Gero Rio
MAP P6 ■ Av Vieira Souto 80, Ipanema ■ (21) 3202 4030 ■ Opening times vary, call ahead ■ $$$
Featuring minimalist decor, Gero Rio *(see p52)* serves fine Italian cuisine.

8 New Natural
MAP N5 ■ Rua Barão da Torre 173, Ipanema ■ (21) 2247 9363 ■ Open 7am–9pm Sat–Thu (until 7pm Fri) ■ $$
A vegetarian *por kilo* restaurant offering soups, salads, and soya casseroles.

9 Brewteco
MAP E6 ■ Rua Dias Ferreira 420, Shop E, Leblon ■ (21) 3217 8280 ■ Open 11:30am–1am Tue–Sun ■ $
Traditional *boteco* with a contemporary style specializing in craft beers and *petiscos* plus *feijoada* on weekends.

10 Esplanada Grill
MAP M5 ■ Rua Barão da Torre 600, Ipanema ■ (21) 2512 2970 ■ Opening times vary, call ahead ■ $$$
For decades, this venue *(see p53)* has been serving superb meat dishes.

Zazá Bistrô Tropical

📺 Western Beaches

Since the 1960s, Rio has been spreading west, boosted by the construction of the Olympic Park on the shore of the revitalized Lagoa de Jacarepaguá. From São Conrado through Barra da Tijuca to Recreio dos Bandeirantes are 12 miles (20 km) of some of the city's most beautiful and unspoiled beaches, with pounding waves drawing the city's top surfers. Lining the area's broad avenues are upscale residential complexes, dozens of shopping malls, and giant arenas. Nevertheless, you can escape the crowds at the pristine wildlife reserves and parks, or several fascinating specialist museums.

Statue of Sítio Roberto Burle Marx

Parque de Marapendi, surrounding Lagoa de Marapendi

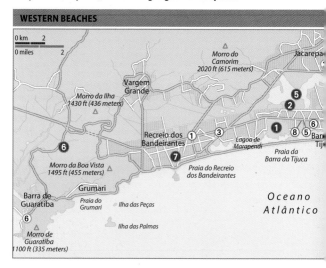

1 Parque de Marapendi
MAP B6 ■ Av Alfredo Baltazar da Silveira, Recreio dos Bandeirantes ■ Open 8am–5pm Tue–Sun

Bordering the narrow lagoon that runs parallel to the Praia de Recreio, this wildlife reserve comprises mangroves and *restinga* (sandbanks), home to waterbirds and other native species. Two paths run through the park, one leading to the Lagoa de Marapendi.

2 Museu do Pontal
MAP B6 ■ Av Celia Ribeiro da Silva Mendes 3300, Barra ■ (21) 2490 2429 ■ Open 10am–6pm Thu–Sun ■ Adm (advance booking required) ■ www.museudopontal.org.br

Home to the largest collection of folk art in Brazil, this specialist museum is one of Rio's lesser-known gems. Thousands of quirky ceramic and wooden figurines are arranged thematically in an airy modern building, which was purpose-built and opened to the public in late 2021. The charming tableaux cover all aspects of rural and city life, such as a football match, a car workshop, and a Carnaval parade. It even has graphically explicit erotic exhibits in an adults-only section.

Barra da Tijuca from Pedra da Gávea

3 Barra da Tijuca
MAP B6

The booming Barra da Tijuca area *(see p40)* is spread along the city's longest beach, whose huge Atlantic breakers make it popular with surfers. With its giant shopping malls, wide avenues, and gated condominiums, Barra looks more like an American neighborhood than a Brazilian one.

4 Cidade das Artes
MAP B6 ■ Av das Américas 5300, Barra da Tijuca ■ (21) 3325 0102 ■ Open 9am–6:30pm daily (later during performances) ■ www.cidadedasartes.rio.rj.gov.br

Barra's huge arts and entertainment complex was nearly 10 years in the making, finally opening in 2013, by which time its budget had rocketed to R$515 million (US$250 million). Designed by eminent French architect Christian Portzamparc, the angular concrete building houses the 1,800-seat home of the Brazilian Symphony Orchestra, as well as other smaller performance halls, an art gallery, cinemas, shops, and restaurants.

Anil

Morro da Cocanha
3205 ft (976 meters)

Itanhangá

São Conrado M

2 miles (3 km)

8

8 Lagoa da Tijuca

São Conrado 4

10

10

Jardim Oceânico M

Joá

Praia de São Conrado 4

5

3

7

Praia da Barra da Tijuca

1

Praia da Joatinga

1	**Top 10 Sights** see pp97–9
1	**Places to Eat** see p101
1	**Shopping Malls** see p100

Lagoa de Jacarepaguá with Barra da Tijuca behind

5 Lagoa de Jacarepaguá
MAP B6 ■ Barra da Tijuca

Lying between Barra da Tijuca and one of Rio's biggest *favelas*, Cidade de Deus, this lagoon is the site of the 2016 Rio Olympic Park. The lagoon's borders are adorned with mangrove and marsh plants.

6 Sítio Roberto Burle Marx
MAP A6 ■ Estrada Roberto Burle Marx 2019, Barra de Guaratiba ■ (21) 2410 1412 ■ Open 9:30–11:30am & 1:30–3:30pm Tue–Sat (guided tour only, advance notice required) ■ sitio burlemarx.blogspot.com.br

These lush landscaped gardens and house *(see p46)* were the home of Roberto Burle Marx, Brazilian landscape designer, who was responsible for much of Rio's modern cityscape, including the iconic wavy pavement mosaics along Copacabana Beach *(see pp30–31)*.

BIODIVERSITY

The Mata Atlântica, or Atlantic coastal rain forest, is isolated from other major South American rain forests by the continent's arid interior, and therefore many of this area's diverse plant and animal species exist only here. Today, less than eight percent of the original forest is left and Brazilians are beginning to realize that eco-tourism is crucial for the rain forest's survival.

7 Parque Ecológico Chico Mendes
MAP A6 ■ Av Jarbas de Carvalho 679, Recreio dos Bandeirantes ■ (21) 2437 6400 ■ Open 8am–5pm Tue–Sun (summer: until 6pm)

This ecological reserve comprises an area of marshes and *restinga* (sandbanks) typical of this low-lying region. Named after Brazilian environmentalist Francisco Alves Mendes, who was murdered in 1988, the park is home to many varieties of endangered plants and animals, including the yellow-throated caiman and three-toed sloth. Trails lead to a small lagoon and an observation tower offers good bird-watching and views over the flat landscape.

Garden, Sítio Roberto Burle Marx

Barra shopping mall
Museu Casa do Pontal
Cidade das Artes
Sítio Roberto Burle Marx
Parque Ecológico Chico Mendes
Praia de Barra da Tijuca
Guaratiba

▶ MORNING

Start the day with a bike ride on the cycle paths beside **Praia de Barra da Tijuca**. Bicycles can be rented from Bike Rio *(see p105)* – a city-wide rental service. Dotted along the seafront are snack stalls where you can stop for a chilled *agua de coco* (coconut water) drunk straight from the shell, and watch the surfers tackle huge rollers coming in off the Atlantic Ocean. Continue to **Parque Ecológico Chico Mendes** in Recreio dos Bandeirantes, for a walk around its mangroves, looking out for caiman and other protected wild-life. Return your bike, then sit down to lunch at one of the area's renowned outdoor seafood restaurants *(see p101)* overlooking the marshes of **Guaratiba**.

AFTERNOON

In the afternoon, take a guided tour around the magnificent house and gardens of **Sítio Roberto Burle Marx** which feature open-air nurseries home to around 3,500 plant species. Afterwards, admire some traditional Brazilian folk art including sculptures, models, and mechanized sets, and learn about Rio's fascinating cultural history at the wonderful **Museu do Pontal** *(see p97)*. In the evening, you can take your pick from one of the dozens of restaurants offering all manner of dishes in the **Barra shopping mall** *(see p100)* for a quick dinner. Round out the day with a concert at the stunning **Cidade das Artes** *(see p97)*, a cultural center housed inside a building suspended 33-ft- (10-m-) above the ground.

⑧ Parque da Cidade
MAP B6 ■ Estrada Santa Marinha, Gávea ■ **(21) 2259 9295** ■ Open 9am–5pm daily

These hillside gardens, bordering Tijuca National Park, were the estate of the Marquês de São Vicente, a 19th-century politician. His former home is now Rio's city history museum, but the park's lawns and ornamental pond are a peaceful spot for a stroll, with great sea views.

⑨ Bosque da Barra
MAP B6 ■ Av das Americas 6000, Barra ■ **(21) 3325 0302** ■ Open 6am–5pm Tue–Sun

This marshy wildlife reserve lies in the center of Barra, flanked by two of the district's busiest thoroughfares. The park shelters a wide variety of waterbirds and animals, including caiman and capybara, the world's largest rodent. Trails and cycle paths run through the park, which also has a playground, volleyball courts, football pitches, and an outdoor gym.

⑩ Praia de São Conrado
MAP B6

Sitting between Leblon and Barra beaches, Praia de São Conrado is one of Rio's top surfing beaches, with waves averaging 3–5 ft (1–1.5 m). The anvil-shaped peak, Pedra da Gávea, towering over the east end of the beach, is popular with rock climbers. The west end, known as Praia do Pepino, is a popular landing spot for hang-gliders taking off from Pedra Bonita. It is essential to check if the water is safe for bathing.

See map on pp97–9 ⟵

Shopping Malls

1 Américas Shopping
MAP B6 ■ Av das Américas 15500 ■ (21) 2442 9902 ■ Open 10am–10pm Mon–Sat (from 11am Sun) ■ www.americasshopping.com.br

Recreio's mall has 240 stores, plus a 12-screen cinema and an ice-rink.

2 Barra Shopping
MAP B6 ■ Av das Américas 4666 ■ (21) 4003 4131 ■ Open 10am–10pm Mon–Sat, 1–9pm Sun ■ www.barrashopping.com.br

Brazil's biggest mall with more than 700 stores and many restaurants.

3 Barra World
MAP B6 ■ Alfredo Baltazar Silveira 580 ■ (21) 3388 6228 ■ Open 10am– 10pm Mon–Sat, 3–9pm Sun ■ barraworld.com

This family-friendly shopping mall provides a variety of free entertainment during the week.

4 Downtown
MAP B6 ■ Av das Américas 500 ■ (21) 2494 7072 ■ Open 8am–10pm Mon–Sat, 1–9pm Sun ■ downtown.com.br

A city within the city, open-air streets are lined with shops, restaurants, and a cinema.

5 Village Mall
MAP B6 ■ Av das Américas 3900 ■ (21) 3003 4177 ■ Open 10am–10pm Mon–Sat, 2–8pm Sun ■ www.shoppingvillagemall.com.br

One of Rio's newest malls, Village Mall is firmly upscale, featuring numerous branded fashion stores, fine-dining options, a fun-filled children's play area, a cinema, and the 1,060-seat Teatro Bradesco.

6 Millennium
MAP B6 ■ Av das Américas 7707 ■ (21) 2438 8220 ■ Open 10am–10pm Mon–Sat, 2–8pm Sun ■ www.shoppingmillennium.com.br

Family-centric Millennium specializes in everything for the house and home, and also has a pet shop.

7 New York City Center
MAP B6 ■ Av das Américas 5000 ■ (21) 3089 1051 ■ Open 10am–10pm Mon–Sat, 1–9pm Sun ■ www.barrashopping.com.br/newyorkcitycenter

This mall has a wide range of stores, as well as restaurants, a cinema, and a four-storey sports center.

8 Rio Design Barra
MAP B6 ■ Av das Américas 7777 ■ (21) 2430 3024 ■ Open 10am–10pm Mon–Sat, 1–9pm Sun ■ www.riodesignbarra.com.br

Focusing on beauty and fashion, this mall has 155 stores, plus three cinemas and a cycle speed training gym.

9 Via Parque
MAP B6 ■ Av Ayrton Senna 3000 ■ (21) 2430 5100 ■ Open 10am–10pm Mon–Sat, 1–9pm Sun ■ viaparqueshopping.com.br

Offering the complete retail experience, including CitiBank Hall, one of Rio's largest concert venues.

10 Fashion Mall
MAP B6 ■ Estrada da Gávea 899 ■ (21) 2111 4444 ■ Open 10am–10pm Mon–Sat, 2–8pm Sun ■ www.fashionmall.com.br

Specializing in high-end designer fashion, this luxurious mall has 120 stores representing the best Brazilian and international brands, as well as gourmet restaurants, cinema, and theater.

Village Mall, Barra da Tijuca

Places to Eat

1 Barraca do Pepê
MAP B6 ■ Av do Pepê, Quiosque 11, Barra da Tijuca ■ (21) 9755 09820 ■ Open 9:30am–7pm daily ■ $

A *Carioca* surfers' institution featuring great sandwiches and smoothies.

2 Benkei Asiático
MAP B5 ■ Shopping Metropolitano Barra, Av Abelardo Bueno 1300, Barra da Tijuca ■ (21) 3325 9812 ■ Open noon–10pm daily ■ $

Choose between dishes from Japan to India at this one-of-a-kind venue.

3 Tourão
MAP B5 ■ Praça São Perpétuo, 116, Barra da Tijuca ■ (21) 2493 4011 ■ Open noon–late daily ■ $$

Not far from Barra Beach, Tourão offers a buffet-style *rodízio* meat feast, with an extensive wine list.

4 QuiQui
MAP B6 ■ Av Prefeito Mendes de Moraes s/n Quiosque 5A/B ■ (21) 99501 0209 ■ Opening times vary, call ahead ■ $

This hip kiosk on Sao Conrado beach has snacks, smoothies, and cocktails.

5 Adegão Português
MAP B6 ■ Rio Design Mall, Av das Americas 7777, 3rd floor ■ (21) 2438 1178 ■ Open noon–11pm Mon–Sat ■ $$

A Portuguese restaurant offering food with a focus on *bacalhau* (salted cod).

6 Bira de Guaratiba
MAP A6 ■ Estrada da Vendinha, 68 A, Grumari ■ (21) 2410 8304 ■ Open noon–5pm Wed–Sun ■ $$$

A fish and seafood restaurant with views of the Restinga da Marambaia.

7 Sushi da Praça
MAP A6 ■ Av Armando Lombardi 949, Barra de Tijuca ■ (21) 2437 0066 ■ Open 6pm–midnight Tue–Fri (from noon Sun) ■ $

This Japanese buffet restaurant attracts a young local crowd.

PRICE CATEGORIES
For a three-course meal for one with half a bottle of wine, taxes and extra charges. Prices are quoted in US dollars.

$ under $25 $$ $25–50 $$$ over $50

---

8 Pobre Juan
MAP B6 ■ Village Mall, Av das Américas 3900, 301 Barra de Tijuca ■ (21) 3252 2637 ■ Open noon–11pm daily ■ $$$

This steakhouse has won many awards for both its fine cuisine and wine list.

Pobre Juan in Fashion Mall

9 Rio Brasa
MAP B6 ■ Av Ayrton Senna 2541, Barra da Tijuca ■ (21) 2199 9191 ■ Open noon–11pm Mon–Sat (until 10pm Sun) ■ $$$

This buffet-style *churrascaria* offers a range of international meat and seafood dishes.

10 Nolita
MAP B6 ■ Village Mall, Av das Américas 3900, Barra de Tijuca ■ (21) 3252 2678 ■ Open noon–11pm Mon–Sat ■ $$

Nolita offers contemporary cuisine, with a particular specialty in stone-baked pizzas.

See map on pp96–7

Streetsmart

The colorful Escadaria Selarón, Lapa

Getting Around	**104**
Practical Information	**106**
Places to Stay	**112**
General Index	**118**
Acknowledgments	**124**
Phrase Book	**126**

Getting Around

Arriving by Air

The popular city of Rio de Janeiro is served by **Tom Jobim/Galeão International Airport** and **Santos Dumont**, for domestic flights.

Rio's international airport, which lies 9 miles (15 km) north of the city center, is often referred to by its former name, Galeão, among locals. It also handles some domestic flights. The airport offers many services, including a Riotur information center, 24-hour ATMs, a post office, shops, and a currency exchange office. Taxis and shuttle buses connect to the city and the domestic airport, Santos Dumont. Taxis to the Ipanema and Copacabana areas cost approximately US$35 from the international airport. Allow at least an hour to get there during the busy rush hours within the city center.

The best airport buses are the **Premium** air-conditioned buses, which leave from airport terminals 1 and 2 and connect to the city center bus station (**Rodoviária Novo Rio**), Aeroporto Santos Dumont, Flamengo, Botafogo, Copacabana, Ipanema, Gávea, Glória, São Conrado, and Barra da Tijuca. Departures are usually every 30 minutes between 6am and 11pm, with a single one-way ticket costing about US$5.

Convenient connections are available across an extensive network of domestic flights, which is often the preferred mode of transportation for a country as large as Brazil. Rio's domestic airport Santos Dumont lies half a mile (1 km) south of the city center. It has a number of shuttle flights to São Paulo on offer as well as onward connections to many of Brazil's other state capitals and major cities. Taxis to Ipanema and Copacabana are around US$15 from here. The Premium bus 2145 connects the two airports as well as the city center.

Arriving by Bus

Efficient and reliable long-distance buses serve the whole country, with luxury express options available on many of the major routes. Arriving into Rio by coach is an easy, comfortable, and economical way to travel and see more of Brazil at the same time. Intercity bus stations, called *rodoviárias*, are usually located on city outskirts. Buses are operated by numerous private companies, but prices are standardized, and usually very reasonable. **Busca Ônibus** is a good source for checking popular routes, as is the **Buses in Brazil** website.

Several categories of buses operate on longer routes; most also have onboard toilets. Regular buses (*ônibus comum*) sometimes do not have air-conditioning, so check beforehand. *Comum com ar* are regular buses with air-conditioning. The *executivo* bus is more comfortable – the seats are normally wider, recline back further, and are equipped with footrests. The best buses for overnight trips are known as *semi-leito* or *leito*. *Semi-leito* have seats that recline almost horizontally and have large footrests. *Leito* buses offer a fully horizontal seat. Both normally have onboard refreshments, blankets, and pillows. It is more convenient to buy your tickets online or direct from the *rodoviária* ahead of time, which is especially recommended for any travel planned around public holidays.

International and interstate buses leave from Rio's downtown bus station, Rodoviária Novo Rio. There is a Riotur information booth (for hotel bookings), a police station, a left luggage office, ATMs, money exchanges, shops, a post office, and a number of cafés. Taxis to the Ipanema and Copacabana areas from here cost around US$18. Take sensible precautions outside the bus station, as the area attracts thieves.

Public Transport

In most Brazilian cities and towns, the main mode of transportation is the bus. Tickets are generally cheap and services run from early morning until late at night. Rio also has a modern metro system on offer, which is often the most convenient means of public transportation around town, as well as plentiful taxis.

Agencia Nacional de Transportes Terrestres is Brazil's main public transport authority. Information on safety and hygiene measures, timetables, tickets and fares, transport maps, and more are readily available online.

Bus

Rio city buses, run by **Rio Onibus**, are numerous and inexpensive. The city's buses operate daily from the early morning until late at night, with some lines running a 24-hour service (with fewer circulating in the middle of the night). Buses are clearly labeled with their destination on the front of the vehicle; to alight, you'll need to flag the bus down at the stop.

Most buses going from the south to the center will go to Copacabana. Brazilian bus drivers can drive fast, and the buses can often be crowded, slow and frequently get stuck in traffic jams. They are also the target of thieves, particularly during the busier rush hours. Buses are best avoided when getting to and from the airport with luggage as well as at night, when petty theft is more common.

Metro

Rio's metro system, **MetrôRio**, has three lines with a total of 41 stations, plus connecting

feeder bus services. It is a safe, clean, reliable, and cheap way to get to many tourist attractions. Lines 1 and 2 run from the north to Ipanema through the city center. Line 4, an extension of Line 1, connects Ipanema and Barra da Tijuca in the west in about 20 minutes.

Tram

The tram or light rail service – **VLT** –links the Rodoviária Novo Rio to the city center via three routes: Line 1, terminating at Santos Dumont airport, Line 2, ending at Praça XV, and Line 3 running from Santos Dumont to Central do Brasil, urban rail station. Tram fares can only be paid using a rechargeable card, which can be bought and charged with credit at all VLT stops.

Tickets

Metro tickets for a single journey (unitário) are available for buses and metros, but not for the VLT trams, for which you must buy a rechargeable card. The Bilhete Único contactless smart cards are sold at stations and can be topped up with cash or bank card, online, or via the PicPay smart-phone app, saving time and money. The rechargeable card can then also be used on bus and metro services thoughout the city. Alternatively, bus tickets can also be bought on board from a ticket seller or the driver.

A range of combined metro-bus-train tickets can also be bought; passengers must ask

for a special integrated ticket (integração) at the time of purchase. These tickets offer useful connections on air-conditioned buses to many of the city's attractions that are off the metro system, such as Sugar Loaf and Ipanema. Free metro maps are also widely available via phone apps and at most ticket booths.

DIRECTORY

ARRIVING BY AIR
Tom Jobim/Galeão International Airport
w riogaleao.com/en

Premium
w aeroportogaleao.net/en/galeao-airport-bus-service

Rodoviária Novo Rio
w novorio.com.br

Santos Dumont
w aeroportosantosdumont.net

ARRIVING BY BUS
Busca Ônibus
w buscaonibus.com.br

Buses in Brazil
w busbrazil.com

PUBLIC TRANSPORT
Agencia Nacional de Transportes Terrestres
w gov.br/antt/pt-br/assuntos/passageiros

BUS
Rio Onibus
w onibus.rio

METRO
MetrôRio
w metrorio.com.br

TRAM
VLT
w vltrio.rio.com.br

Ferry

Given the country's abundant rivers and coastline, in many parts of Brazil boats and other water vehicles are a vital form of transport. From Rio, a cheap ferry service connects the city to the municipality of Niterói, and beyond to the island of Ilha Grande and the municipality of Angra dos Reis. **CCR Barcas** ferries depart from downtown Rio de Janeiro at the Praça XV de Novembro, with departures leaving every 15 to 20 minutes most days (6:30–10am and 4:40–8pm Mon–Fri, 5:30am–11:30pm Sat and Sun). The journey from Rio to Niterói (Praça Araribóia) takes about 20 minutes.

Taxi

Used frequently by locals, taxis are a comfortable way of getting around Rio, and they're not necessarily the most expensive form of transport if, for instance, you share a ride to the airport. Standard (comum) licensed yellow-and-blue taxis are the most common on the streets of Rio. These taxis use a two-tariff meter system, indicated by a flag on the dashboard. Tariff 1 is all day up to 10pm; tariff 2 applies after 10pm, all day Sundays, and also on public holidays. While all licensed taxis operate from hotels or the taxi stands in each neighborhood, not all of those hailed on the streets are from a cooperative service. Some reliable taxi cooperatives you can use include **Aerocoop** and

Transcoopass. The taxi service **Especial Coop Taxi RJ** is a good option for those travelling with specific requirements.

Another option, more commonly used among the locals, is the motorcycle taxi (or *moto-taxi*, as it's known throughout the country). This mode of transport, for one person, is cheap and fast, and it's more common in smaller towns. The driver carries an extra helmet for the passenger, who just hops onto the back and rides pillion after agreeing a fixed price for the journey.

Driving

Driving in Rio is one of the least favored ways to get around the city. There are many confusing one-way systems on the roads, and traffic is very chaotic, with long tailbacks during peak hours, and traffic jams that can be horrendous. Brazilians can also be somewhat aggressive drivers: many will drive fast, switch lanes often (normally without any signaling), and tend to overtake. Parking, expecially in cities, can be particularly tricky, as there are often security concerns and significant space constraints. If you are planning to drive while staying in Rio, it is worth considering accommodation with a lock-up garage facility (although these are usually the more expensive options). Never leave valuables in the car. Generally, it is wise to avoid driving around the city after dark.

Rotas Brasil is an excellent tool to use when planning your journey, as it provides detailed information on best routes, approximate distances, tolls, and traffic rules.

In general, most of the vehicles in Brazil run on either gasoline or hydrous alcohol. Service stations selling gasoline are common throughout the country, especially in more remote areas. When leaving Rio on long distance trips, service stations may be few and far between, so ensure that you have enough fuel and that the car is in good condition.

Car Rental

Renting a car in Rio can be costly, so it is worth organizing a deal before leaving for Brazil. Most major car rentals are represented in the city and also have offices at the airports. These include both the main international companies, as well as Brazilian firms such as **Localiza**, **Movida**, and **Unidas**, which are all popular options for car rental.

Foreigners looking to rent a car in Brazil will need to show a valid driver's license from their home country, province, or state; a valid passport; and a major credit card. It is also a good idea to carry an International Driver's Permit (IDP) if this is available to you.

Rules of the Road

Cars are always driven on the right side of the road in Brazil. Right turns on red lights are not allowed and roundabouts are common only in Brasília. The right of way is always with the car on the roundabout, or to the left. On highways, keep headlights and seatbelts on otherwise there is a risk of being fined. Traveling by night is usually best avoided – with few exceptions, highways are poorly lit and lacking in reflective paint, reflective signage, and reflectors showing the edge of the road.

The speed limit on the highway *(autopista)* is 68 mph (110 km/h), while on rural roads the speed limit is set at 50 mph (80 km/h) and in urban areas it is 37 mph (60 km/h).

All drivers are also legally obliged to carry an emergency triangle and a fire extinguisher with them. In the case of an emergency, it is best to call the **Polícia Rodoviária** (Highway Police).

Cycling

With its vast size, tropical climate, and highspeed road network, Brazil is not usually considered an ideal location for more intense, long-distance cycling. However, the cities are a good option for shorter rides. In Rio de Janeiro, cycling is becoming a popular form of transport, and there has been a rise in the number of bicycle lanes alongside the beaches, and around the Lagoa Rodrigo de Freitas. It's now possible to find bike hire companies in many of Rio's beach-side neighborhoods, while the

government-sponsored **Bike Sampa** service offers thousands of orange bicycles *(tembici)* to rent from access points citywide. These bikes are available for hire by the hour, day, or longer, with many useful suggested routes available online. For a more leisurely option, there are also a number of pleasant organized bike tours to be enjoyed around the city, offered by companies including **Baja Bikes**.

Walking and Hiking

In many ways, Rio is the perfect city for walkers, with its miles of sandy beaches, wide expanse of shady parks and gardens, and a friendly outdoor city culture. During the day, the city center, Lapa, and Santa Teresa, as well as the beach neighborhoods of Leblon, Ipanema, and Copacabana, are ideal for getting around on foot, with street cafes, museums, and galleries abundant in these areas. The best way to explore the city on foot is to use public transport to get to the areas of interest and then walk from there. Joining a walking tour is also a great option, especially if you wish to visit a *favela* – look for tour groups that contribute part of their income to the community.

With plenty of nature and viewpoints around the city, Rio has a number of good hiking trails. Hiking in Rio can be suited to varying experience levels, so always check the route online or at the tourist office for more infor-

mation and plan before heading out. As with any outdoor adventure, bring provisions, wear weather-appropriate clothing, and tell someone where you're going and when you plan to return. It's always important to leave no trace: this could be as simple as taking your litter home with you, not disturbing wildlife, or keeping to paths in order to prevent any damage to fragile flora.

Practical Information

Passports and Visas

For entry requirements, including visas, consult your nearest Brazilian embassy or check the **Polícia Federal** website. Brazil operates a reciprocal visa policy; as such, citizens of the UK, EU, Australia, New Zealand, US, Canada, Japan, Mexico, and South Africa do not need a visa, provided they have a return ticket and their stay in Brazil does not exceed 90 days.

Government Advice

Now more than ever, it is important to consult both your and the **Brazilian Government's** advice before travelling. The **UK Foreign, Commonwealth & Development Office**, the **US State Department** and the **Australian Department of Foreign Affairs and Trade** offer the latest information on security, health, and local regulations.

Customs Information

You can find information on the laws relating to goods and currency taken in or out of Brazil by checking the information available on the Brazilian Government's website.

Travel Insurance

We recommend taking out a comprehensive insurance policy covering theft, loss of belongings, medical care, cancellations, and delays, and read the small print carefully.

Health

Brazil has a universal public health system. Emergency medical treatment in public hospitals is available for foreign nationals, while private hospitals will require proof of funds and insurance. It is therefore important to arrange comprehensive medical insurance before travelling. There are some private medical centers that have English speaking staff, including **Hospital Samaritano** and **Clínica Galdino Campos**.

Food and drink hygiene is good in most major tourist areas. Tap water should be avoided, but bottled water is available for purchase everywhere. *Farmácias* (pharmacies) such as **Drogaria Cristal**, **Drogaria Wilson**, **Farma Life**, or **Drogaria Pacheco** can be found throughout Rio, some of which are open 24 hours. The **DisqueAids** helpline is available for those seeking advice on HIV, AIDS, and STDs.

Dengue fever and zika are present in the country. Both viral diseases are transmitted mainly by mosquitoes, and there are no vaccines to prevent them. Symptoms include high fever, joint pain, headaches, and, for zika, a rash. Zika may be more serious for pregnant women, with evidence it causes birth defects. Use mosquito repellent, especially between dusk and dawn.

Ask your doctor or a travel clinic for an International Certificate of Vaccinations, an up-to-date list of required vaccinations. The most often recommended are a DTP (diptheria, tetanus, and polio) booster, as well as vaccinations for typhoid and hepatitis A. Yellow fever vaccination is highly recommended, especially if you are planning to visit rural areas; visitors can be asked to provide a yellow fever vaccination certificate upon entering the country. For information regarding COVID-19 vaccination requirements, consult government advice.

Smoking, Alcohol and Drugs

Smoking is more widely tolerated here than in the US and in Europe, although it is prohibited on public transport. Drink driving is strictly banned, with regular police checks. Be aware that even a small amount of alcohol in the blood may lead to a prison sentence. It is always best to exercise caution when someone unknown offers you a drink or even cigarettes. Instances of drugging drinks are not uncommon. Severe penalties, including prison, are enforced for possession of illegal drugs.

ID

It is mandatory in Brazil to carry some form of photo identification. You may be asked to show some form of ID when entering an office building or government agency, or sometimes even a museum or library. To avoid carrying around a passport, keep a photocopy, and carry another, less valuable form of ID that has your picture, name, and date of birth.

Personal Security

Although much of Rio de Janeiro is safe for visitors, petty crime does occur. Use your common sense (such as storing valuables in a safe at your accommodation, wearing a money belt, and using ATMS inside banks, malls, and supermarkets where possible) and be alert to your surroundings, and you should enjoy a trouble-free trip. If out at night, favor licensed taxis instead of walking long distances or taking the bus.

If you are a victim of a crime, contact the police as soon as possible,

ideally within 24 hours. You will need to ask for a *boletim de ocorrência* (incident report form), which will be needed in order to make a claim. **DEAT** (which stands for Delegacia Especial de Apolio Ao Turismo) is Rio's English-speaking tourist police unit, based in Leblon at the far end of Ipanema. At other police stations, generally only Portuguese is spoken. For emergencies, contact the **police**, **fire department** or **ambulance service**.

If you wish to visit a *favela*, it's recommended that you go with a local guide and choose a tour that contributes to the local community.

By and large, Rio is considered a welcoming and open-minded city. It's probably the most LGBTQ+-friendly place in Brazil, with bars and nightclubs along the Copacabana and Ipanema beaches – particularly

along Rua Farme Amoeda – popular meeting places for the local gay community. The **International LGBTQ+ Travel Association** provides useful information online for both Rio and the rest of Brazil. A regular LGBTQ+ event that takes place in the city is Rio Pride (one of the 150 to take place throughout the country), while the annual *carnaval* has become increasingly LGBTQ+-friendly.

That said, Brazil is also known for its macho culture; members of the LGBTQ+ community and women may encounter unsolicited comments as a result. Wearing a wedding ring or traveling in a group can be a disincentive. Should you feel unsafe, ignore any unwanted attention and keep to busy areas with other people around.

DIRECTORY

PASSPORTS AND VISAS

Brazil Polícia Federal
w pf.gov.br

GOVERNMENT ADVICE

Australia Department of Foreign Affairs and Trade
w smartraveller.gov.au

Brazilian Government
w gov.br/mre/en

UK Foreign, Commonwealth & Development Office
w gov.uk/world/brazil

US State Department
w travel.state.gov

HEALTH

Clínica Galdino Campos
MAP R3 ■ Av NS. de Copacabana 492
w clinicagaldino campos.com.br

DisqueAids
■ Open 8:30am–5:30pm Mon–Fri
c 0800 541 0197

Drogaria Cristal
MAP H3 ■ Rua Marquês de Abrantes 27, Flamengo
c (21) 2265 3444

Drogaria Pacheco
MAP Q4 ■ Av N. Sra. de Copacabana 534,
w drogarias pacheco.com.br

Drogaria Wilson
MAP L5 ■ Av Henrique Dumont 85, Ipanema
c (21) 2249 7000

Farma Life
MAP B6 ■ Barra Shopping mall, Av das Américas 4666, shop 115
c (21) 4002 2000

Hospital Samaritano
MAP G4 ■ Rua Bambina 98, Botafogo
w botafogo.hospital samaritano.com.br

PERSONAL SECURITY

Ambulance (Ambulância)
c 192

DEAT
MAP L5 ■ Rua Humberto de Campos 315
c (21) 2332 2924

Fire Department (Bombeiros)
c 193

Police (Polícia)
c 190

International LGBTQ+ Travel Association
w iglta.org

Travelers with Specific Requirements

Although it is relatively easy to find accessible hotels and restaurants, older buildings may lack elevators or ramps, and streets and sidewalks are often uneven. Many metro stations have accessible entries, tactile paving and hearing loops. **Especial Coop** taxis have specially adapted cars and English-speaking drivers, and the **Society for Accessible Travel and Hospitality (SATH)** offers useful tips on its website.

Time Zone

Rio is on Brazilian Standard Time, with daylight saving runing from the third Sunday in October to the third Sunday in February.

Money

The Brazilian currency is the *real* (R$). The only foreign currencies commonly accepted are the US dollar and euro.

For safety reasons, some ATMs (*caixas automáticas*) limit cash withdrawals after 10pm until 6am; it is best try to use them during the day. Credit cards are widely accepted, and contactless payments are gradually becoming more common. Tipping is not normally expected unless added in advance to the bill.

Electrical Appliances

The power sockets used here are type N for three-pin plugs, or type C for two-pronged plugs. The standard voltage is 127 or 220 volts AC.

Cell Phones and Wi-Fi

Most international networks have roaming contracts with Brazil. Dialing charges can be high, with expensive rates for receiving calls from outside Rio state. You can opt to buy a local SIM card on arrival; the pay-as-you-go *(pre-pago)* deals are likely the best options available.

For long-distance calls, dial the three- or four-digit code of a *prestadora* (service provider) before the area or country code. You can use any provider; the most common are **Vivo** (15), **Claro** (21), **Tim** (41), and **Oi** (31).

There are plenty of cafés with Internet in Rio, while most hotels offer Wi-Fi for guests.

Postal Services

Correios (post offices) are widespread. Postcards are cheap, but the system of pricing for letters and parcels sent to Europe or the USA is complex – prices can vary greatly from office to office and clerk to clerk. Express deliveries are known as SEDEX; for valuable items, international couriers, such as Fedex and DHL, are more reliable.

Weather

Rio is beautiful at any time of the year. It is wet and warm from November to February, and dry and sunny during the rest of the year. The most popular times to visit are December and during Carnaval, which usually falls in February or March. Bring clothing for temperatures that can range from 95°F (35°C) to 59°F (15°C). Rio is an informal city; suits and ties are rare, for example. Flipflops (*chinelos* or *havaianas*) or sandals are commonly worn in beach neighborhoods, while walking shoes are good for the city center and for forest walks. Leave expensive watches, smartphones, and jewelry at home.

Opening Hours

Banks are open on weekdays from 9am or 10am until 3pm or 4pm, but currency exchanges often stay open an hour later. Post office timings vary but they are usually open from 9am to 5pm. Shops are open from 9am until 6pm from Monday to Saturday, and malls stay open in the week from 10am until 10 or 11pm, later on Saturdays, and some on Sunday afternoons too.

The **COVID-19** pandemic proved that situations can change suddenly. Always check before visiting attractions and hospitality venues for up-to-date hours and booking requirements.

Visitor Information

Riotur, the city's official tourist authority, has information booths dotted all over Rio. Its website has updated information in English, highlighting the major attractions, as well as nightlife, entertainment, hotels, and restaurants. **Rio Carnaval** offers tickets, information, and advice for carnaval-goers.

Useful information can also be found on the official **Brazilian Tourism** website. Rio's English-language news site, **The Rio Times**, is a good guide to what's on in the city and beyond.

Local Customs

Brazilians tend to be friendly and open. Good friends will embrace upon meeting, and, when they are introduced for the first time, people shake hands, give a friendly slap on the shoulder, or offer a kiss on the cheek. Casual dress is the norm in Rio, even in smart hotels and restaurants; business suits are only needed for work and formal meetings. Nudity or going topless on the beach, however, is not accepted anywhere, apart from when on a number of designated naturist beaches.

Most churches and cathedrals permit visitors during Sunday mass; some historic monuments charge entry. Although Brazil is known to have a traditionally strong Catholic identity, Afro-Brazilian religions such as Candomblé are widely practised. When visiting religious buildings, always ensure that you are dressed modestly, with both your knees and shoulders well covered.

Responsible Tourism

Before booking any organized tours, it is advisable to find out whether they are locally run, contribute to the local community, and encourage responsible waste collection. Protect local wildlife by not removing any plants or rocks, and only observing animals from a distance.

Language

Portuguese is the official language in Brazil, but several Indigenous languages are also spoken. Social niceties are important, so starting a conversation with "bom dia" will go a long way. Locals may speak some English in tourist areas, but in general, English is not widely spoken.

Taxes and Refunds

There are no VAT refunds included in the price of purchases. Departure taxes are usually included in international airfares, but it is advisable to check with your airline or travel agent.

Accommodation

Rio has a range of places to stay, from luxury beach resorts to hostels. The majority of hotels are located in Copacabana, Ipanema, and Leblon; accommodation is more expensive, but much of the best dining, nightlife, and shopping is concentrated around this area, plus it is generally safer. Many international chains dot the beach-front districts, while some of the more characterful boutique hotels and B&Bs can be found around Santa Teresa and Gávea.

Furnished apartments from agencies such as **Rio Exclusive**, **Rio Holidays**, or **Homes in Rio** are an excellent money-saving option; most can be rented for a week or more.

It is essential to book in advance for the peak seasons: from Christmas to Carnaval (usually taking place in February or early March), as well as for July and August.

DIRECTORY

TRAVELERS WITH SPECIFIC REQUIREMENTS

Especial Coop
W especialcoop.com.br

SATH
W sath.org

CELL PHONES AND WI-FI

Claro
W claro.com.br

Oi
W oi.com.br

Tim
W tim.com.br

Vivo
W vivo.com.br

VISITOR INFORMATION

Brazilian Tourism
W visitbrazil.com

Rio Carnaval
W rio-carnival.net

The Rio Times
W riotimesonline.com

Riotur
W riotur.rio/en

ACCOMMODATION

Homes in Rio
W homesinrio.com

Rio Exclusive
W rioexclusive.com

Rio Holidays
W rioholidays.com

Places to Stay

PRICE CATEGORIES
For a standard, double room per night (with breakfast if included), taxes, and extra charges.

$ under US$85 $$ US$85–$200 $$$ over US$200

Luxury Hotels

Intercity Porto Maravilha
MAP G1 ▪ Rua Cordeiro da Graça 598, Santo Cristo ▪ (21) 2195 1385 ▪ www.intercityhoteis.com.br ▪ $
Set inside a gleaming modern tower with spectacular views over Porto Maravilha and Guanabara Bay, this is a sophisticated hotel in a prime location. Amenities here include a rooftop pool, basement parking, and an excellent buffet breakfast.

Windsor Guanabara
MAP W2 ▪ Av Presidente Vargas 392, Centro ▪ (21) 2195 6000 ▪ www.windsorhoteis.com/hotel/windsor-guanabara ▪ $
Located close to the city center, across the street from Candelária Church, this flagship of the Windsor chain offers spacious rooms, a fitness center, and a swimming pool.

Sol Ipanema
MAP M6 ▪ Av Viera Souto 320, Ipanema ▪ (21) 2525 2020 ▪ www.solipanema.com.br ▪ $$
This beachside four-star hotel has an infinity pool as well as a terrace bar. The higher floors are quieter and offer views of the ocean. Facilities include an Italian restaurant, a fitness center and a beauty parlor. A buffet breakfast is included in the price of the room.

Windsor Barra
MAP B6 ▪ Avenida Lucio Costa 2630, Barra da Tijuca ▪ (21) 2195 5000 ▪ www.windsorhoteis.com.br ▪ $$
This five-star modern, business-oriented hotel overlooks Barra da Tijuca beach; with spacious bedrooms, conference center, and rooftop pool with striking views.

Wyndham Rio de Janeiro Barra
MAP B6 ▪ Av Lúcio Costa 3150, Barra da Tijuca ▪ (21) 3139 8000 ▪ www.wyndhamhotels.com ▪ $$
These twin towers right on the beach are the best choice for stays in the neighborhoods of Barra da Tijuca and Recreio dos Bandeirantes. The rooms are spacious and have balconies with sea views.

Copacabana Palace
MAP R3 ▪ Av Atlântica 1702, Copacabana ▪ (21) 2548 7070 ▪ www.copacabanapalace.com.br ▪ $$$
Copacabana's most famous and plush hotel, Copacabana Palace features ocean-view suites that have housed princes, presidents, and visiting film stars. Portraits of many of the famous guests can be seen in the gallery. The older portion of the hotel is renowned for having the best rooms.

Fasano
MAP P6 ▪ Av Vieira Souto 80, Ipanema ▪ (21) 3202 4000 ▪ www.fasano.com.br ▪ $$$
A world-class luxury accommodation situated in Ipanema and designed by Philippe Starck with a 1950s "Bossa Nova" look. The rooms are beautifully appointed with marble bathrooms and most have private balconies with sea views. The restaurant here is excellent, as is the rooftop infinity pool. There is also a salon spa, dedicated to holistic wellness, on the hotel's first floor.

Hilton Copacabana
MAP H5 ▪ Av Atlantica 1020, Copacabana ▪ (21) 3501 8000 ▪ www.hilton.com ▪ $$$
A classic Hilton offering, this hotel is housed inside a towering building right on the seafront. There's a rooftop pool, a cocktail bar, as well as a range of delightful luxury treats including complimentary happy hour drinks in the hotel's executive lounge.

Hotel Emiliano
MAP Q5 ▪ Av Atlantica 3804, Copacabana ▪ (21) 3503 6600 ▪ www.emiliano.com.br ▪ $$$
São Paulo-based designer hotel chain's latest addition, Emiliano stands out amid Copacabana's otherwise traditional beachfront. The rooms here are light and airy, furnished with wooden flooring. There is also a superb in-house restaurant and a rooftop pool here, alongside a host of other plush amenities.

Marina Palace
MAP L6 ■ Av Delfim
Moreira 630, Leblon ■ (21)
2529 5700 ■ www.hotel-
marina-rio-leblon.h-rez.
com ■ $$$
One of the better tower
hotels, the Marina Palace
is within walking distance
of Leblon's restaurants
and has 150 spacious
rooms, free Wi-Fi, a pool,
and a sauna. The upper
floors offer great views
of the ocean.

Pestana Rio Atlântica
MAP Q4 ■ Av Atlântica
2964, Copacabana
■ (21) 3816 8500 ■ www.
pestana.com ■ $$
The views of Copacabana
from this hotel's rooftop
pool are some of the best
in Rio. The rooms all have
private balconies.

PortoBay Rio Internacional
MAP R3 ■ Av Atlântica
1500, Copacabana
■ (21) 2546 8000 ■ www.
portobay.com ■ $$
Ideally located for
beach enthusiasts, this
Copacabana seafront
hotel has a rooftop pool
and rooms with great
views of the sea as well
as the beach.

Boutique and Designer Hotels

yoo2 Rio de Janeiro
MAP H4 ■ Praia de
Botafogo 242 ■ (21) 3445
2000 ■ www.yoo2.com
■ $$
Facing Botafogo Beach,
this stylish modern hotel
has four rooms and one
suite, each with minimalist
decor. There's also a rooftop bar, a restaurant, spa,
and a range of tours
available, from cocktail
mixology to canoeing.

Casa Áurea
MAP V6 ■ Rua Áurea 80,
Santa Teresa ■ (21) 2242
5830 ■ $
This family-run budget
boutique hostel sits in its
own little garden patio on
a Santa Teresa backstreet.
Each room is different
and is decorated with art.
The crowd is young and
the staff is fluent in
multiple languages,
including English.

Rio Design
MAP Q5 ■ Rua Francisco
Sá 17, Copacabana
■ (21) 3222 8800 ■ www.
riodesignhotel.com ■ $
Copacabana's first
designer-led boutique
hotel has 84 individually
styled suites in a business-
like, tall, narrow tower. The
decor is minimalist, the
furnishings are functional,
and the service attentive.

Gávea Tropical
MAP E6 ■ Rua Sérgio
Pôrto 85, Gávea ■ (21)
97547 0939 ■ www.
boutiquehotelgavea
tropical.getawayrentals.
info ■ $
This modern boutique
hotel offers stunning views
of Gávea and Corcovado
and is conveniently located
close to Ipanema and
Leblon's beaches. The
hotel's three rooms and
villa feature an Asian-
tropical decor, and guests
can enjoy amenities such
as an outdoor pool, sauna,
spa, and fitness center.

Le Relais de Marambaia
MAP A6 ■ Estrada Roberto
Burle Marx 9346, Barra de
Guaratiba ■ (21) 2394
2544 ■ www.lerelaisde
marambaia.com.br ■ $$
A rarity among the
high-rise complexes

typical of Barra, this
luxurious French-run
boutique hotel ticks all
the boxes for a hideaway
haven. It has three rooms
and four suites, each with
a balcony; a restaurant,
pool and spa, and a
lovely terrace overlooking
the ocean.

Marina All Suites
MAP L6 ■ Av Delfim
Moreira 696, Leblon
■ (21) 2172 1001 ■ $$
This plush sea-front
hotel, which has hosted
many celebrities, features
17 signature suites
created by leading
designers. It also offers
22 additional suites with
lounges and home
heaters, and has a great
bar and restaurant.

Casa Mosquito
MAP G6 ■ 222, Rua Saint
Roman, Copacabana
■ (21) 3586 5042 ■ $$$
Located up a steep
winding street overlooking
Copacabana and
Ipanema, this beautiful
boutique hotel has nine
stylish suites featuring
retro decor of the 1950s,
including four that are
inspired by famous
Cariocas. A spa and
outdoor pool add to its
luxurious touches.

Hotel Santa Teresa
MAP V6 ■ Rua Almirante
Alexandrino 660, Santa
Teresa ■ (21) 3380 0200
■ www.santateresahotel
rio.com ■ $$$
The most exclusive
boutique hotel in Santa
Teresa; luxurious suites
with hardwood flooring
and designer furniture,
plus spa and tropical gardens; its Térèze French
restaurant is one of the
finest in Rio.

La Suite

MAP B6 ▪ Rua Jackson de Figueiredo 501, Joá ▪ (21) 3259 6123 ▪ www. bydussol.com ▪ $$$
Rio's finest boutique hotel overlooks the exclusive Joatinga beach. Each of its eight rooms and suites is painted a different color and has a lush marble bathroom to match.

Mama Ruisa

MAP V6 ▪ Rua Santa Cristina 132, Santa Teresa ▪ (21) 98885 0631 ▪ www. mamaruisa.com ▪ $$$
A charming boutique hotel housed in a converted 18th-century mansion house in Santa Teresa luxuriously furnished with antiques and original artworks. Each room here is named after a French or Brazilian cultural icon, including Josephine Baker and Carmen Miranda, with decor to match.

Mid-Priced Hotels

55/RIO

MAP Q4 ▪ Av Atlântica 3564, Copacabana ▪ (21) 3883 2030 ▪ $
With jaw-dropping views over Copacabana from its top-floor restaurant, this is a modest beachfront hotel featuring bright, airy rooms. Some suites have living areas with sofas, armchairs, as well as hardwood dining tables.

Casa Cool Beans

MAP U6 ▪ Rua Laurinda Santos Lobo 136, Santa Teresa ▪ (21) 2262 0552 ▪ www.casacoolbeans. com ▪ $
This delightful B&B is spread over four floors and offers ten luxurious, tastefully decorated guest rooms which have

en-suite bathrooms, air conditioning, a mini bar, and complimentary Wi-Fi access. Other facilities at the hotel include a swimming pool, gardens, and a sundeck. A complimentary Brazilian-style breakfast is also offered.

Copacabana Mar

MAP R3 ▪ Rua Min. Viveiros de Castro 155, Copacabana ▪ (21) 3501 7900 ▪ www.hotel copacabanamar.com.br ▪ $
This beach-front tower has comfortable rooms with minimalist, neutral decor and king-size beds. The hotel's business facilities are modern with free access to wireless Internet in all rooms.

Regina

MAP H3 ▪ Rua Ferreira Viana 29, Flamengo ▪ (21) 3289 9999 ▪ www.hotel regina.com.br ▪ $
This solid, old hotel is tucked away in one of Flamengo's quieter side streets and features small but clean modern rooms, with free Wi-Fi access. The buffet breakfasts are good and its location offers easy access to downtown and the beaches.

Savoy Othon Travel

MAP Q4 ▪ Av Nossa Senhora de Copacabana 995 ▪ (21) 2125 0200 ▪ www.othon.com.br ▪ $
Clean and comfortable, the Savoy is part of the prosperous Brazilian Othon chain, but its rates are significantly lower than many similar hotels in the area. Its rooftop restaurant and the rooms on the upper floors provide fantastic views of Copacabana.

Windsor Flórida

MAP H3 ▪ Rua Ferreira Viana 81, Catete ▪ (21) 2195 6800 ▪ www. windsorhoteis.com.br ▪ $
This centrally located hotel has more than 400 well-appointed rooms and a master suite on each floor, plus a pool and fitness center. The roof-top terrace here offers impressive views of Flamengo Beach and Sugar Loaf Mountain.

Hotel Vermont

MAP N5 ▪ Rua Visconde de Pirajá 254, Ipanema ▪ (21) 3202 5500 ▪ www. hotelvermont.com.br ▪ $$
The better rooms in this hotel are on the higher floors and have decent views, while the rooms on the lower floors overlook a concrete wall. This is one of the mid-priced options in town and is popular with the LGBTQ+ community.

Ipanema Inn

MAP N6 ▪ Rua Maria Quiteria 27, Ipanema ▪ (21) 2523 6092 ▪ www. ipanemainn.com.br ▪ $$
There are good beach views from the upper floors of this towering building, which is tucked behind the Sofitel Ipanema hotel. The hotel has plain but well-maintained rooms, and is close to Ipanema beach and popular shopping streets.

Mar Ipanema

MAP M5 ▪ Rua Visconde de Pirajá 539, Ipanema ▪ (21) 3875 9191 ▪ www. maripanema.com ▪ $$
This tower lies in the heart of Ipanema, near the beach and shopping areas. The simple rooms have wooden floors and black and white prints of Rio.

Quinta Azul

MAP V6 ▪ Rua Almirante Alexandrino 256, Santa Teresa ▪ (21) 3253 1021 ▪ $$

Housed in a blue-painted colonial building, this centrally located boutique *pousada* has chic, modern rooms decorated with antique furniture. Some rooms have balconies overlooking the hills of the neighborhood.

Apartments and Houses

Jucati Season Apartments

MAP Q3 ▪ Rua Tenente Marones de Gusmão 85, Copacabana ▪ (21) 2547 5422 ▪ www.edificio jucati.com.br ▪ $

Rent by the day or the week at this bargain-priced apartment block, around 10 minutes' walk from Copacabana Beach. Each modestly sized apartment has one double bed, two bunk beds and a kitchenette.

WhereInRio

www.whereinrio.com ▪ $$$

This company provides luxury penthouses and villas for holiday rental (minimum 3 nights), in Rio and along the coast from Búzios to Paraty. The service is excellent with concierge, boat charter, and airport transfers available.

Copa Apartments

MAP Q4 ▪ Rua Figueiredo de Magalhães 144, Copacabana ▪ (21) 3268 5264 ▪ www.copa apartments.com ▪ $$

A Brazilian family-run vacation rental agency that offers apartments of various sizes, in Copacabana and Leme, with housekeeping services and tour guides, should you need them.

Copacabana One Flat

MAP P4 ▪ Rua Pompeu Loureiro 99, Copacabana ▪ (21) 3500 1960 ▪ www. copaoneflat.com ▪ $$

These modest apartments offer a concierge service, a pool, sauna, laundry, and a garage. They are located six blocks away from both Copacabana and Ipanema beaches near Lagoa Rodrigo de Freitas.

Residencial Meridiano Arpoador

MAP P6 ▪ Rua Francisco Otaviano 61, Ipanema ▪ (21) 2113 8600 ▪ $$

With pleasant facilities including a fitness suite, an outdoor pool and a sauna, this hotel offers spacious self-catering apartments, each with a fitted kitchen.

The Brazil Beach House Company

(84) 99993 8936 ▪ www.brazilbeach house.com ▪ $$$

This British-run company offers luxurious beach and town houses throughout Rio de Janeiro, as well as some beautiful properties in Búzios, Paraty, and elsewhere around Brazil.

Copacabana Holiday

MAP R3 ▪ Rua Barata Ribeiro 90A, Copacabana ▪ (21) 2542 1525 ▪ www. copacabanaholiday.com. br ▪ $$

Offering between one to four bedrooms, these rental apartments are found in Copacabana, Ipanema, and Leblon, and many of them are situated right along the beach front, with glorious ocean vistas. Some of the locations are very good value.

Rio Luxury Apartments

(21) 4042 4903 ▪ www. rioluxuryapartments.com ▪ $$

This multilingual outfit has a large collection of apartments for short and long-term rental, along the coast from Leme to Barra de Tijuca. They sleep from two to six, and many have private balconies and breathtaking beach views.

Homes in Rio

▪ (21) 9863 30846 ▪ www. homesinrio.com ▪ $$$

A German-based firm offering long- and short-term luxury apartment rentals, including penthouses. Properties are located across the city, from Botafogo to Gávea, particularly in desirable beach areas.

Rio Exclusive

▪ (21) 99293 2081 ▪ www. rioexclusive.com ▪ $$$

Based in downtown Rio, this agency rents out luxury apartments, houses as well as private island accommodation all over Rio and also beyond to Buzios and Costa Verde.

Budget Hotels and Hostels

Atlantis Copacabana

MAP P5 ▪ Rua Bulhões de Carvalho 61, Copacabana ▪ (21) 2521 1142 ▪ www. atlantis hotel.com.br ▪ $

Small but comfortable air-conditioned rooms, and a two-minute walk from Copacabana and Ipanema beaches make this a sought-after accommodation.

For a key to hotel price categories see p112

Babilônia Rio Hostel
MAP S2 ■ Ladeira Ari Barroso 50, Babilônia ■ (21) 3873 6826 ■ www.babiloniariohostel.com.br ■ $

Getting to this cool, bright hostel situated in a small *favela* above Leme involves a bit of a climb, but the great ocean view and easy-going atmosphere make it worth the effort.

Beach House Ipanema
Rua Barao da Torre 485 ■ (21) 3202 2693 ■ www.beachhouseipanema.com ■ $

Only a few blocks from Ipanema beach and at a close proximity to many restaurants and clubs, this welcoming hostel boasts a fun, laid-back vibe. On site, there is a pretty little garden, a bar and a pool. Some of the rooms here have their own private bathroom.

Che Lagarto Hostel
MAP M5 ■ Rua Paul Redfern 48, Ipanema ■ (21) 97415 2730 ■ www.chelagarto.com ■ $

Ideal for solo travelers and backpackers and set in an unbeatable location, this clean and efficient hostel is among the four branches of the South American chain across Ipanema and Copacabana. Facilities include an on-site bar and communal kitchen, free Wi-Fi, and air conditioning.

Jo&Joe Hostel
MAP G3 ■ Beco do Boticario 26, Cosme Velho ■ (21) 3235 2600 ■ $

This fun and lively hostel has an ideal location near Novo Rio bus station and the Corcovado funicular.

It offers a range of private rooms and dorms, plus a communal kitchen, restaurant, bar and a small pool in the patio garden.

Hotel Vitoria
MAP H3 ■ Rua do Catete 172, Catete ■ (21) 2557 0159 ■ www.vitoriariode janeirohotellaris.com ■ $

Located in the Flamengo neighborhood, this functional but good-value hotel is just across the road from Catete Palace and Republic Museum Garden – perfect for a leisurely stroll.

Ibis Botafogo
MAP G4 ■ Rua Rua Paulino Fernandes 39, Botafogo ■ (21) 3515 2999 ■ www.allaccor.com/hotel/7547 ■ $

This small hostel, which has a tiny back patio and a little bar, is one of the very few cheap options in Leblon. It occupies a converted town house with four- and six-bed dormitories, which include a women-only dormitory.

Mango Tree Hostel
MAP N5 ■ Rua Prudente de Morais 594, Ipanema ■ (21) 3281 3021 ■ www.mango treeipanema.com ■ $

Situated in the heart of Ipanema, just a block away from the beach, this place is a good choice if you are seeking a hostel with airy dorms, private rooms, and a host of activities.

Margarida's Pousada
MAP M5 ■ Rua Barão da Torre 600, Ipanema ■ (21) 2239 1840 ■ www.mar garidaspousada.com ■ $

This little family-run guesthouse at the quiet end of Ipanema has 11

suites and two family-size apartments on offer. The friendly owners and the staff go out of their way to make the guests feel at home. Advance booking is recommended.

The Maze
MAP H3 ■ 414, Rua Tavares Bastos, Catete ■ (21) 2558 5547 ■ www.mazerio.com.br ■ $

This arty hostel is situated in one of the city's safest *favelas*, Tavares Bastos, and offers both private rooms as well as dorm beds. Brit expat owner Bob Nadkarni is famously welcoming, and on the first Friday of the month visitors can enjoy live jazz and *bossa nova* on its terrace that overlooks Guanabara Bay.

Rio Forest Hostel
MAP V5 ■ Rua Joaquim Murtinho 517, Santa Teresa ■ (21) 3563 1020 ■ $

This converted old mansion offers private rooms or dorm beds. It is split-level with lots of stairs, and has a pool and bar on an airy terrace offering superb views over Santa Teresa. There's a basic kitchen and a good buffet breakfast is available.

SESC Copacabana
MAP Q4 ■ Rua Domingos Ferreira 160, Copacabana ■ (21) 4020 2101 ■ www.sescrio.org.br ■ $$

This cultural center, built in a style made famous by the Brazilian architect Oscar Niemeyer (see p72), features a theater, cinema, and hotel just one block from the beach. The atmosphere is quiet and the rooms are clean, modern, and very well maintained.

Hotels in Rio State

Hotel Chalés Terra Nova

MAP A2 ■ Estrada do Parque Nacional Km 4.5, Parque Nacional do Itatiaia ■ (24) 98828 8714 ■ www.hotelchalesterra nova.com.br ■ $

With suites and charming *cabanas* situated on the edge of the lush green rainforest, this hotel features a pool in a peacock- and hummingbird-filled tropical garden. The hotel also organizes a number of light adventure activities for guests.

Abracadabra

MAP C2 ■ Rua Morro do Humaitá 13, Búzios ■ (22) 2623 1217 ■ www. abracadabrapousada. com.br ■ $$

This establishment offers the same enviable views out over Búzios and the Atlantic as its sister hotel, Casas Brancas. It is just five minutes from the bustling Rua das Pedras and offers a range of both simple and reasonably-priced rooms as well as luxury suites.

Casas Brancas

MAP C2 ■ Rua Morro do Humaitá 8, Búzios ■ (22) 2623 0303 ■ www.casas brancas.com.br ■ $$

Búzios's plushest hotel comprises a series of mock-Moorish villas on the side of a hill overlooking the Atlantic and the Ilha Branca. The town center and many shops and restaurants are just a walk away, and beach buggies are available for hire. The hotel has an excellent spa, an infinity pool, and a restaurant serving gourmet food.

Pousada Bromelias

MAP A2 ■ Estrada da Grauna, Km 562, Paraty ■ (24) 3512 5710 ■ www. pousadabromelias. com.br ■ $$

Featuring luxury *cabanas* set in the heart of the Mata Atlântica rain forest, this hotel spa offers a range of relaxing treatments, from *reiki* to aromatherapy massage. The hotel has a pool, tennis courts, and a decent restaurant.

Pousada da Alcobaça

MAP B2 ■ Rua Agostino Goulão 298, Correas, Petrópolis ■ (24) 2221 1240 ■ www.pousadada alcobaca.com.br ■ $$

This enchanting *pousada* near Petrópolis offers 11 tastefully furnished rooms in an early 20th-century house, set amid magnificent grounds complete with a pool, tennis court, and nature trail. Gourmet meals, focusing on organic produce from the pousada's adjacent vegetable garden are available.

Pousada do Sandi

MAP A2 ■ Largo do Rosário 1, Paraty ■ (24) 3371 2100 ■ www.sandi hotel.com.br ■ $$

The most comfortable and well appointed of all the *pousadas* in Paraty's colonial center has a spa, a good restaurant, and a bar serving *caipirinhas*.

Sagu Mini-Resort

MAP A2 ■ Praia da Bica, Abraão, Ilha Grande ■ (24) 3361 5823 ■ www.casa-da-ilha-inn-sagu-mini-resort.negocio.site ■ $$

At this romantic island hideaway, nine rooms with balconies and surrounded by tropical gardens overlook Abraão Bay. Facilities include a restaurant, breakfast, kayaks, massages, and a solar-heated hot tub.

Solar do Império

MAP B2 ■ Av Koeler 376, Petrópolis ■ (24) 2103 3000 ■ www.solardo imperio.com.br ■ $$

The most luxurious hotel in Petrópolis is housed in a classically furnished 19th-century mansion on the city's grandest avenue. Facilities include air-conditioned rooms, a chic restaurant, outdoor and indoor pool, and a spa.

Pousada Literária de Paraty

MAP A2 ■ Rua do Comércio 362, Paraty ■ (11) 2770 0237 ■ www. pousadaliteraria.com.br ■ $$$

This hotel offers a set of luxuriously fitted rooms facing an outdoor pool or fully detached villas, including one overlooking the bay. The two suites located on the upper floor are among some of the best rooms in town.

Pousada Picinguaba

MAP A3 ■ Rua G Picinguaba 130, Vila Picinguaba ■ (12) 99637 7173 ■ www.weare nature.com/picinguaba ■ $$$

This gorgeous retreat has nine tastefully decorated rooms and a three-bed villa in the Serra do Mar forest reserve, one of the most beautiful and well-preserved stretches of Brazilian coastline. Activities include private schooner cruises, guided jungle treks, and snorkeling in the bay.

For a key to hotel price categories see p112

General Index

Page numbers in **bold**
refer to main entries.

A

Accommodation 110–17
  boutique and designer
    hotels 113–14
  budget 57, 115–16
  Copacabana Palace 30,
    58, 95, 112
  hostels 57
  hotels 111
  luxury hotels 112–13
  mid-priced hotels 114–15
  rental 111, 115
  in Rio State 117
Air travel 104
Américo, Pedro
  Batalha do Avaí 20
Anima Mundi – Festival
  Internacional de Cinema
  de Animacão 61
Architecture 72
Arcos da Lapa 84
Arpoador Beach 40
Art galleries *see* Museums
  and galleries

B

Baile Vermelho e Preto do
  Flamengo (Carnaval) 59
Baixo Bebê 49
Banda de Ipanema
  (Carnaval) 58
Banks 108, 109
Barra da Tijuca 40, 97
Bars and Nightclubs **50–51**
  Botecos (Botequins) 66,
    68, 76, 80, 83, 87
  Centro district 68
  Confeitaria Colombo 52,
    68
  Copacabana, Ipanema
    and Leblon
    neighborhoods 33, 92
  Corcovado 12
  Garota de Ipanema 92
  Jardim Botânico 25, 49
  Lagoa, Gávea, and
    Jardim Botânico
    neighborhoods 76, 80
    map 76
  Santa Teresa and Lapa
    neighborhoods 83, 86
  Sugar Loaf Mountain 16
  Travessa do Comércio 29
  Western Beaches 100

Beach exercise 32
Beach massage 33
Beach soccer 30, 45
Beach volleyball 32, 42
Beaches 40–41, 56, 110
  Arpoador 40
  Barra da Tijuca 40
  Botafogo 40
  Charitas 40
  Farme 32
  Flamengo 41
  Grumari 41
  Guanabara Bay beach
    neighborhoods 72, 74
  Ipanema 6, 11, **32–3**, 40,
    42, 58, 91
  Leblon 11, **32–3**, 40, 91
  postos 33
  Praia de Copacabana 11,
    30–31, 40, 43, 60, 91
  Praia de Fora 72
  Praia de São Conrado 40,
    99
  Praia Vermelha 47, 74
  Recreio dos
    Bandeirantes 41
  sand sculptures 33
Beachwear 32, 108
  shops 54
Bicycles 105
Biggs, Ronnie 84
BioParque do Rio 49
Bloco Cacique de Ramos
  (Carnaval) 58
Bloco de Segunda
  (Carnaval) 58
Blocos 58–9
Boats and ships
  Estacão das Barcas 28
  ferry dock 28, 104–5
  Marina da Glória 74
  Porto Maravilha 67
Bosque da Barra 99
Bossa nova 93
Botafogo (Soccer Club) 44
Botafogo beach 40
Botecos (Botequins) 66
  Centro district 68
  Lagoa, Gávea, and
    Jardim Botânico
    neighborhoods 76, 80
  Santa Teresa and Lapa
    neighborhoods 83, 87
Brasilia 37
Brecheret, Victor
  Portadora de Perfumes
    20

Budget tips 57
Burle Marx, Roberto 46, 98
Bus travel 104
Búzios 47

C

Cabo Frio 47
Candelária church 66
Capoeira 56
Carnaval 58–9, 60
  costumes 55
  Santa Teresa 58, 83
Cars and driving 105
  car hire 105
  licenses 109
Casa de Arte e Cultura
  Julieta de Serpa 74
Casa de Cultura Laura
  Alvim 92
Casa de Rui Barbosa 73
Cascatinha do Taunay 14
Castelinho do Flamengo 74
Catedral Metropolitana de
  São Sebastião 57, 66
Centro 64–9
  Candelária Church 66
  Confeitaria Colombo 52,
    68
  Igreja Santo Antonio 66
  itinerary 67
  map 64, 67
  Mosteiro de São Bento
    10, **18–19**, 65
  Museu Histórico Nacional
    11, **26–7**, 38, 65
  Museu Nacional de
    Belas Artes 10, **20–21**,
    38, 65
  Porto Maravilha 67
  Praça XV 11, **28–9**, 65
  restaurants 69
Chácara do Céu 83
Chafariz da Glória 74
Chafariz do Mestre
  Valentim 29
Champions' Parade
  (Carnaval) 58
Chapel of the Santissimo
  19
Charitas beach 40
Children
  Baixo Bebê 49
  BioParque do Rio 49
  Jardim Botânico 11,
    24–5, 49
  Museu do Pontal 46,
    49, 97

Children (cont.)
Parque da Catacumba 48, 77
Parque das Ruínas 48
Parque Guinle 74
Parque Nacional da Tijuca 10, **14–15**, 46, 48
Planetário 49, 79
play areas 49
Rodrigo de Freitas Lagoon 49
Sugar Loaf Mountain 10, **16–17**, 48, 71, 73
Churches and abbeys 57
Candelária Church 66
Catedral Metropolitana de São Sebastião 57, 66
Centro district 65, 66
chapel at the base of Cristo Redentor 13
Chapel of the Santissimo 19
Guanabara Bay beach neighborhoods 71
Igreja da Ordem Terceira de Nossa Senhora do Monte do Carmo 29, 65
Igreja de Nossa Senhora do Carmo da Antiga Sé 28, 65
Igreja Nossa Senhora da Glória do Outeiro 71
Igreja Santa Cruz dos Militare 28
Igreja Santo Antonio 66
Mayrink Chapel 15
Mosteiro de São Bento **18–19**, 65
Cidade das Artes 97
Circo Voador 85
Confeitaria Colombo 52, 68
Constant, Benjamin 84
Convento de Santa Teresa 84
Copacabana, Ipanema and Leblon neighborhoods 31, 90–95
Casa de Cultura Laura Alvim 92
Copacabana Palace 30, 58, 95, 112
Dois Irmãos 91
Feira Hippie Market 54, 94
Garota de Ipanema 92
Ipanema 11, **32–3**, 40, 42, 91
itinerary 93
Leblon 11, **32–3**, 40, 91
map 90–91, 93
Morro da Leme 31, 92

Copacabana, Ipanema and Leblon neighborhoods (cont.)
Museu da Imagem e da Som 93
Museu H. Stern 93
Praia de Copacabana 11, **30–31**, 40, 43, 60, 91
restaurants 92, 95
Rua Dias Ferreira 92
shopping 91, 94
Corcovado 7, 8–9, 10, **12–13**, 78
COVID-19 109
Cristo Redentor 7, 8–9, 12–13
Cunhambebe, Chief 37
Currency 108
Customs regulations 106

D

Da Conceicão, Frei Domingos 18
Da Fonseca, Edgar de Oliveira 66
Da Fonseca, Marechal Deodoro 37
De Almeida, Belmiro *Arrufos* 20
De Lemos, Gaspar 36, 37
De Sá, Estácio 72
De Sá, Mem 37
De Villegagnon, Admiral Nicolas Durand 36, 37
Deodoro Olympic Park 43
Dia do Índio 61
Diving 43
Do Amaral, Tarsila 21
Dois Irmãos 91
Dom João VI, King 36
Dom Pedro I, Emperor 36, 37
Dom Pedro II, Emperor 37, 71
statue 26
Driving licenses 109

E

Electrical appliances 109
Emergency Services 107
Escadaria Selarón 56, 84
Estacão das Barcas 28
Estádio do Maracanã 39, 43, 44

F

Farme beach 32
Favelas 78, 98, 105, 107
tours 110, 111
Feira de São Cristóvão 47, 54, 57

Feira do Rio Antigo 85
Feira Hippie Market 54, 94
Ferry dock 28, 104–5
Festa de Nossa Senhora da Penha 61
Festa de São Sebastião 60
Festa Literária Internacional de Paraty 60–61
Festival Internacional de Cinema do Rio 61
Festivals and shows 60–61
Carnaval 55, 58–9, 60
New Year's Eve 30, 61
Fifa World Cup 37
Film and cinema
Anima Mundi – Festival Internacional de Cinema de Animacão 60–61
Festival Internacional de Cinema do Rio 61
Fishers 31
Fitness *see* Sports
Flamengo (Soccer Club) 44
Flamengo beach 41
Floresta da Tijuca 14
Fluminense (soccer club) 44
Football *see* Soccer
Fortaleza de Santa Cruz 46
Fortaleza de São João 74
Forte de Copacabana 30
Forte do Leme *see* Forte Duque de Caxias
Forte Duque de Caxias 30
Free attractions 56–7
see also Museums and Galleries
French explorers 36
French-Tamoio Alliance 36
Fundação Eva Klabin 77
Futevolei 32, 45

G

Gala Gay at Rio Scala (Carnaval) 59
Garota de Ipanema 92
Gávea 43
see also Lagoa, Gávea, and Jardim Botânico neighborhoods
The Girl from Ipanema (Vinícius de Moraes and Antônio Carlos Jobim) 33, 92
Golf 43
Grumari beach 41
Guanabara Bay Beach neighborhoods 70–75

Guanabara Bay Beach
neighborhoods (cont.)
Casa de Arte e Cultura
Julieta de Serpa 74
Casa de Rui Barbosa 73
Castelinho do Flamengo
74
Chafariz da Glória 74
Fortaleza de São João 74
Guanabara Bay 16, 36,
37, 38
hiking trails 73
Igreja Nossa Senhora da
Glória do Outeiro 71
itinerary 73
map 70, 73
Marina da Glória 74
Memorial Getúlio Vargas
74
Monumento Nacional
aos Mortos da II
Guerra Mundial (War
Memorial) 71
Morro da Urca 16, 17, 48,
73
Museu de Folclore
Edison Carneiro 72
Museu do Índio 72
Museu Villa-Lobos 72
Oi Futuro Flamengo 74
Parque do Flamengo 74
Parque Guinle 74
Pista Cláudio Coutinho 73
Praça Paris 71
Praia Vermelha 47, 74
restaurants 75
Sugar Loaf Mountain 10,
16–17, 48, 71, 73

H
Hang-gliding 14, 42
Health 106
Hiking 43
Corcovado 78
Morro do Leme 31, 91
Parque Nacional da
Tijuca 14, 46, 48
Pista Cláudio Coutinho
73
Sugar Loaf Mountain 10,
16–17, 48, 71, 73
History 36–7

I
Igreja da Ordem Terceira
de Nossa Senhora do
Monte do Carmo 29, 65
Igreja de Nossa Senhora
do Carmo da Antiga Sé
28, 65

Igreja Nossa Senhora da
Glória do Outeiro 71
Igreja Santa Cruz dos
Militare 28
Igreja Santo Antonio 66
Ilha Fiscal 39
Ilha Grande 46, 47
Immigration 106
Indigenous people 72
Instituto Moreira Salles 77
Internet 108
Ipanema 11, **32–3,** 40, 42, 91
Banda de Ipanema 58
see also Copacabana,
Ipanema and Leblon
neighborhoods
Itineraries
a climb up Morro da
Urca and the Sugar
Loaf 73
a day at the beach 93
a day in Rio's parks and
gardens 79
a day in the historic
centre 67
a day on Western
Beaches 99
four days in Rio de
Janeiro 7
two days in Rio de
Janeiro 6
two nights of music in
Lapa 85

J
Jardim Botânico 11, **24–5,**
49, 77
João VI of Portugal 37
Jockey Club Brasileiro
79
Juices 41

K
Kite surfing 42
Kubitschek, Juscelino 37

L
Lagoa de Jacarepaguá 98
Lagoa, Gávea, and
Jardim Botânico
Neighborhoods **76–81**
Fundação Eva Klabin 77
Instituto Moreira Salles
77
itinerary 79
Jardim Botânico 11,
24–5, 49, 77
Largo do Boticário 78
map 76, 79
nightlife 80

Lagoa, Gávea, and
Jardim Botânico
neighborhoods (cont.)
Parque da Catacumba
48, 77
Parque do Cantagalo 79
Parque Lage 78
restaurants 81
Rocinha favela 78
Lagoa Rodrigo de Freitas
43
Lapa see Santa Teresa and
Lapa Neighborhoods
Largo das Neves 83
Largo do Boticário 78
Largo dos Guimarães 83
Le Breton, Joaquim 21
Leblon 11, **32–3,** 40, 91
Rua Dias Ferreira 92
see also Copacabana,
Ipanema and Leblon
neighborhoods
Leme (neighbourhood) 31
LGBTQ+ travelers 59, 107

M
Maps
bars and nightclubs 50
Centro 64, 67
Copacabana, Ipanema,
and Leblon
neighborhoods 90–91,
93
Guanabara Bay beach
neighborhoods 70, 73
Lagoa, Gávea, and
Jardim Botânico
neighborhoods 76, 79
restaurants 52
Rio de Janeiro 6–7
Santa Teresa and Lapa
neighborhoods 82, 85
shops and markets 54
Western Beaches 96–7,
99
Maracanã 43
"Maracanaco Tragedy" 45
Maria Lenk Aquatics
Centre 43
Maria, Queen 29
Marina da Glória 43, 74
Mata Atlântica 47
Mayrink Chapel 15
Meirelles, Victor
Primeira Missa no Brasil
20
Memorial Getúlio Vargas
74
Mirante Andaime Pequeno
15

Mirante Dona Marta 15
Monumento Nacional aos
    Mortos da II Guerra
    Mundial (War
    Memorial) 71
Monuments
    Cristo Redentor 7, 8–9,
        10
    Guanabara Bay beach
        neighborhoods 71, 74
    Memorial Getúlio Vargas
        74
    Monumento Nacional
        aos Mortos da
        II Guerra Mundial
        (War Memorial) 71
Morro da Leme 31, 91
Morro da Urca 16, 17, 48,
    73
Mosquitos 106
Mosteiro de São Bento 10,
    18–19, 65
Mountains and monoliths
    Corcovado 7, 8–9, **12–13,**
        78
    Dois Irmãos 91
    Morro da Leme 31, 91
    Pedra Bonita 14
    Pedra da Gávea 15
    Pico da Tujuca 46
    Serra dos Órgãos 47
    Sugar Loaf Mountain 10,
        16–17, 48, 71, 73
Museu Casa Benjamin
    Constant 84
Museu do Pontal 46, 49,
    97
Museu Casa dos Pilões
    25
Museu da Imagem e da
    Som 93
Museu da República 38
Museu de Arte
    Contemporânea de
    Niterói (MAC) 38
Museu de Arte do Rio 67
Museu de Arte Moderna
    (MAM) 39
Museu de Folclore Edison
    Carneiro 72
Museu do Amanhã 38, 66
Museu do Bonde 47
Museu do Índio 72
Museu H. Stern 93
Museu Histórico Nacional
    11, **26–7,** 38, 65
Museu Nacional 39
Museu Nacional de Belas
    Artes 10, **20–21,** 38, 65
Museu Villa-Lobos 72

Museums and galleries
    38–9, 56
    Casa de Cultura Laura
        Alvim 92
    Casa de Rui Barbosa 73
    Centro district 65
    Chácara do Céu 83
    Cidade das Artes 97
    Convento de Santa
        Teresa 84–5
    Estádio do Maracanã 39
    Fundação Eva Klabin 77
    Guanabara Bay beach
        neighborhoods 72–3
    Ilha Fiscal 39
    Lagoa, Gávea, and
        Jardim Botânico
        neighborhoods 77, 79
    map 39, 54
    Museu Casa Benjamin
        Constant 84
    Museu do Pontal
        46, 49, 97
    Museu Casa dos Pilões
        25
    Museu do Amanhã 38, 66
    Museu da Imagem e da
        Som 93
    Museu da República 38
    Museu de Arte
        Contemporânea de
        Niterói (MAC) 38
    Museu de Arte Moderna
        (MAM) 39
    Museu de Folclore
        Edison Carneiro 72
    Museu do Bonde, Santa
        Teresa 47
    Museu do Índio 72
    Museu H. Stern 93
    Museu Histórico
        Nacional 11, **26–7,** 38
    Museu Nacional 39
    Museu Nacional de Belas
        Artes 10, **20–21,** 38, 65
    Museu Villa-Lobos 72
    Planetário 49, 79
    Sambódromo 39
    Santa Teresa and Lapa
        neighborhoods 83, 84,
        85
    Sítio Roberto Burle Marx
        46, 98
    Trem do Corcovado
        Museum 13
Music and dance 57
    bossa nova 93
    capoeira 56
    Cidade das Artes 97
    Circo Voador 85

Music and dance (cont.)
    The Girl from Ipanema
        (Vinícius de Moraes
        and Antônio Carlos
        Jobim) 33, 92
    Heitor Villa-Lobos 72
    live music 61, 80, 86
    Museu da Imagem e da
        Som 93
    Samba schools 59
    Santa Teresa and Lapa
        neighborhoods 85
    shops 94

N

National parks and nature
    reserves 25
    Bosque da Barra 99
    Ilha Grande 46, 47
    Parque Ecológico Chico
        Mendes 46
    Parque Nacional da
        Tijuca 10, **14–15,** 46, 48
    Parque Nacional do
        Itatiaia 47
Newspapers 109
Niemeyer, Oscar 38, 72
Nightlife
    Lagoa, Gávea, and
        Jardim Botânico
        neighborhoods 76, 80
    Santa Teresa and Lapa
        neighborhoods 86
Niterói 46

O

Oi Futuro Flamengo 74
Olympic golf course 43
Olympic venues 43
Opening hours 109
Orquidarium (Jardim
    Botânico) 25
Outdoor activities *see*
    Sports

P

Paço Imperial 28, 29
Palácio Gustavo Capanema
    72
Palácio Tiradentes 28
Pão de Açúcar *see* Sugar
    Loaf Mountain
Paragliding 42
Paraty 47
    Festa Literária
        Internacional de Paraty
        60–61
Parks and gardens 56
    Guanabara Bay beach
        neighborhoods 74

Parks and gardens (cont.)
Jardim Botânico 11,
24–5, 49
Lagoa, Gávea, and
Jardim Botânico
neighborhoods 77, 78,
79
Parque da Catacumba
48, 77
Parque da Cidade 99
Parque das Ruínas 48,
83
Parque de Marapendi 97
Parque do Cantagalo 79
Parque do Flamengo 74
Parque Ecológico Chico
Mendes 98
Parque Guinle 74
Parque Lage 78
Sítio Roberto Burle Marx
46, 98
Parque da Catacumba 48,
77
Parque da Cidade 99
Parque das Ruínas 48, 83
Parque de Marapendi 97
Parque do Cantagalo 79
Parque do Flamengo 74
Parque Ecológico Chico
Mendes 46, 98
Parque Guinle 74
Parque Lage 78
Parque Nacional da Tijuca
10, **14–15**, 46, 48
Parque Nacional do Itatiaia
47
Passports 106
Pedra Bonita 42
Pedra da Gávea 15
Pelé 39, 44, 45
Petrópolis 47
Pico da Tijuca 46
Pilar, Frei Ricardo 18
Pista Cláudio Coutinho 73
Planetário 49, 79
Portinari, Cândido
Café 21
Porto Maravilha 67
Portuguese explorers 36
Portuguese Royal Family
36
Postal services 109
Postos 33
Praça Paris 71
Praça XV 11, **28–9**, 65
Praia de Copacabana 11,
30–31, 40, 43, 60, 91
Praia de São Conrado 40,
99
Praia Vermelha 47, 74

R
Rainforests 47
Recreio dos Bandeirantes
Beach 41
Região dos Lagos 47
Republic (Brazil as) 37
Restaurants 52–53
Botecos (Botequins) 66
Centro district 69
Copacabana, Ipanema
and Leblon
Neighborhoods 92, 95
dining 110
Guanabara Bay beach
neighborhoods 75
Lagoa, Gávea, and
Jardim Botânico
neighborhoods 81
map 52
Os Esquilos (Parque
Nacional da Tijuca) 14
Santa Teresa and Lapa
neighborhoods 87
Western Beaches 100, 101
Rio de Janeiro State
Championship 45
Rio Olympic Arena 43
Rio Olympic Park 43
Rio-vs-São Paulo
Tournament 44–5
Riotour 110
Rocinha Favela 78
Rock climbing 16, 43
Rodin, Auguste
Meditacão Sem Braco 21
Rodrigo de Freitas Lagoon
49
Rua Dias Ferreira 92
Running and jogging 42

S
Samba 85
clubs 86
schools 59
Sambódromo 39, 43
Carnaval 58
Santa Marta Favela 72
Santa Teresa and Lapa
neighborhoods **82–7**
Arcos da Lapa 84
botecos (Botequins) 83, 87
Carnaval 58, 83
Chácara do Céu 83
Circo Voador 85
Convento de Santa
Teresa 84
Escadaria Selarón 56, 84
Feira do Rio Antigo 85
itinerary 85
Largo das Neves 83

Santa Teresa and Lapa
neighborhoods (cont.)
Largo dos Guimarães 83
map 82, 85
Museu Casa Benjamin
Constant 84
Parque das Ruínas 48, 83
restaurants 87
trams 83
Saymos do Egyto
(Carnaval) 59
Security 106
Serra dos Órgãos 47
Shops and markets
antiques and second-
hand 85
beachwear 54
bookshops 55
Copacabana, Ipanema
and Leblon
neighborhoods 91, 94
crafts 54, 55
designer and boutique
91, 101
Feira de São Cristóvão
47, 54, 57
Feira do Rio Antigo 85
Feira Hippie Market 54, 94
jewelry 55, 93
music 94
opening hours 109
Santa Teresa and Lapa
neighborhoods 85
shopping malls 101
Teresópolis 47
western beaches 101
Sítio Roberto Burle Marx
46, 98
Soccer 44–5
clubs 44
Estádio do Maracanã 39,
43, 44
stars 45
Sports 42–3
beach exercise 32
beach soccer 30, 45
beach volleyball 32, 42
cycling and running
tracks 32, 79, 99
diving 43
futevolei 32, 45
golf 43
hang-gliding 14, 42
hiking 14, 16–17, 31, 43,
46, 73, 78
Jockey Club Brasiliero 79
kite surfing 42
Olympic venues 43
paragliding 42
rock climbing 16, 43

Sports (cont.)
running 42
soccer 39, 43, 44–5
surfing 42
windsurfing 42
Squares and fountains
Centro district 65
Chafariz da Glória 74
Chafariz do Mestre
Valentim 29
Guanabara Bay beach
neighborhoods 71, 74
Lagoa, Gávea, and
Jardim Botânico
neighborhoods 78
Largo das Neves 83
Largo do Boticário 78
Largo dos Guimarães
83
Praça Paris 71
Praça XV 11, **28–9,** 65
Santa Teresa and Lapa
neighborhoods 83
St. Benedict 19
St. Theresa 84–5
Sugar Loaf Mountain 10,
16–17, 48, 71, 73
Sunsets and sunrises 12,
56
Surfing 42

T

Taxis 105
Telephones 57, 108,
109
Television 109
Teresópolis 47
Tickets 104
Time difference 109
Tiradentes 28
Tourist information 110,
111
Trains and funiculars
Sugar Loaf Mountain 17,
71
Trem do Corcovado 13
Transport
air travel 104
bicycles 105
bus travel 104
cars and driving 105
MetrôRio 57
sea travel 104
taxis 105
tickets 104
trains and funiculars 13,
17, 71
trams 83, 104
VLT 104
Travel insurance 106

Travelers with specific
needs 108
Travessa do Comércio 29
Trem do Corcovado
Museum 13
Trips and tours 110, 111
walking tours 56

V

Vaccinations 106
Valença, Vale do Café 46
Valentim, Mestre 28, 29
Vargas, Getúlio 37, 38, 74
Vasco da Gama (soccer
club) 44
Views and lookout points
57
Corcovado 7, 8–9, 10,
12–13, 13
Dois Irmãos 91
Fortalza de Santa Cruz 46
Jardim Botânico 24
Mirante Andaime
Pequeno 15
Mirante Dona Marta 15
Morra da Urca 16, 17, 48,
73
Parque da Catacumba
48, 77
Parque do Flamengo 74
Sugar Loaf Mountain 17,
48, 71, 73
Villa-Lobos, Heitor 72
Visas 106
VLT (Veículo Leve sobre
Trilhos) 104

W

Walking 105
tours 56
see also Hiking
Waterfalls
Cascatinha do Taunay 14
Weather 109
Western Beaches **96–101**
Barra da Tijuca 97
bars and cafés 100
Bosque da Barra 99
Cidade das Artes 97
itinerary 99
Lagoa de Jacarepaguá
98
Museu Casa do Pontal
46, 49, 97
Parque de Marapendi 97
Parque Ecológico Chico
Mendes 46, 98
Praia de São Conrado 40,
99
restaurants 100, 101

Western Beaches (cont.)
shopping 101
Sítio Roberto Burle Marx
46, 98
Wildlife and nature
biodiversity 98
BioParque do Rio 49
Bosque da Barra 99
Jardim Botânico 11,
24–5, 49, 77
Lagoa, Gávea, and
Jardim Botânico
neighborhoods 77, 79
Parque de Marapendi 97
Parque Ecológico Chico
Mendes 46, 98
Parque Nacional da
Tijuca **14–15,** 46, 48
Sugar Loaf Mountain 16,
17, 48, 71, 73
Windsurfing 42

Y

YYemanjá 61

Z

Zoos 48

Acknowledgments

This edition updated by

Contributor Huw Hennessy
Senior Editor Alison McGill
Senior Art Editor Vinita Venugopal
Project Editors Dipika Dasgupta, Tijana Todorinovic
Editor Mark Silas
Art Editor Bandana Paul
Picture Research Manager Taiyaba Khatoon
Picture Research Administrator Vagisha Pushp
Publishing Assistant Halima Mohammed
Jacket Designer Jordan Lambley
Cartographer Ashif
Cartography Manager Suresh Kumar
Senior DTP Designer Tanveer Zaidi
Senior Production Editor Jason Little
Senior Production Controller Samantha Cross
Deputy Managing Editor Beverly Smart
Managing Editors Shikha Kulkarni, Hollie Teague
Managing Art Editor Sarah Snelling
Senior Managing Art Editor Priyanka Thakur
Art Director Maxine Pedliham
Publishing Director Georgina Dee

DK would like to thank the following for their contribution to the previous editions: Alex Robinson

The publisher would like to thank the following for their kind permission to reproduce their photographs:
(**Key:** a-above; b-below/bottom; c-centre; f-far; l-left; r-right; t-top)

4Corners: Guido Cozzi 3tr, 102-3; Günter Gräfenhain 3tl, 62-3; SIME/Antonino Bartuccio 2tr, 4t, 4cla, 4crb, 4b, 34-5, 58t, 88-9.

Agency O Globo: Monica Imbuzeiro 19crb.

Alamy Images: A.PAES 61tr; Alexandra 50br; Arco Images/Therin-Weise 19bl; Bjanka Kadic 51crb; bilwissedition Ltd. & Co. KG 37tr; Laura Coelho 25cb; David Davis Photoproductions 22-3; Foto Arena LTDA / Andr Horta 93cla; Hemis.fr./Bertrand Gardel 83cr; © Ildi.Food 41tr; imageBROKER/Florian Kopp 44t; M.Sobreira 55t; JTB Media Creation, Inc. 32-3c; Mountain Light/Galen Rowell 14-5c; MJ Photography 11cra; Old Books Images 36t; Robert Harding World Imagery/Yadid Levy 57tr; Fernando Quevedo de Oliveira 60t.

AWL Images: Peter Adams 56t; Alex Robinson 19tl.

Bar Urca: 75cr.

Bridgeman Images: Dom Pedro II, also known as Magnanimous (Rio de Janeiro, 1831-Paris, 1889), Emperor of Brazil /De Agostini Picture Library 37cl.

Colecao Museu Nacional de Belas Artes/PHAN/MinC: Arrufos by Belmiro de Almeida photo by César Barreto 20cla; Le Manteau Rouge by Tarila do Amaral/www.tarsiladoamaral.com.br photo by Romulo Fialdini 21tl; Primeira Missa no Brasil by Vitor Meireles photo by Jaime Acioli 20clb.

Corbis: Guido Cozzi 18-9c; epa /Antonio Lacerda 59tr; Farrell Grehan 98bl; Yadid Levy 92bl; Alex Robinson 14cl, 54tl.

Dorling Kindersley: Carregadora de perfume by Victor Brecheret ©DACS, London 2015 10br; Colonização e Dependência by Clécio Penedo, Museu Hitstorico Nacional 26cla; Cafe by Candido Portinari © DACS, London 2015 21br; Mural by Candido Portinari in the Instituto Moreira Salles, Instituto Moreira Salles, Gavea ©DACS, London 2015 77t.

Dreamstime.com: Aguino 84bl; Celso Diniz 11bl; Dabldy 59bl, 67clb, 84t; Danflcreativo 38br; Diego Grandi 65br; Alexandre Durão 60bl; Ekaterinabelova 11crb; Filipe Frazao 4clb, 40bl, 92t; Diego Grandi 6ca, 7tr; Lazyllama 45cl; Lindrik 72b; Luizsouzarj 61cl; Mypix 42tl, 78t; Paura 91br; Pixattitude 10clb; Matyas Rehak 52crb; Celso Pupo Rodrigues 43tr, 44bl; Vanessa Rung 47tr; Vincentho 21tl, 8-9; Wideweb 57bl; Zts 36c.

Getty Images: Brazil Photos 98t; Gamma-Keystone/Keystone-France 45tr; Stuart Dee 43cl; Lonely Planet Images/Krzysztof Dydynski 64cla; Luiz Grillo 46cr; Richard I'Anson 4cra.

Guimas Restaurante/Daniella Cavalcanti Assessoria de Imprensa: 81b.

Getty Images / iStock: luoman 42b.

Tyba Photographic Agency: J R Couto 16-7cr.

Zazá Bistrô Tropical: 95b.

Lasai: 53t.

Cover

Front and spine: **Getty Images / iStock:** Diegograndi.

Back: **Alamy Stock Photo:** David Davis Photoproduction cl, Ben Fisher crb, Jon Arnold Images Lt tr; **Getty Images / iStock:** Diegograndi b; **iStockphoto. com:** Shumoff tl.

Pull Out Map Cover
Getty Images / iStock: Diegograndi.

All other images © Dorling Kindersley. For further information see: www.dkimages.com.

Penguin Random House

First Edition 2009

First published in Great Britain by
Dorling Kindersley Limited
DK, One Embassy Gardens, 8 Viaduct Gardens, London SW11 7BW, UK

The authorised representative in the EEA is
Dorling Kindersley Verlag GmbH. Arnulfstr. 124, 80636 Munich, Germany

Published in the United States by
DK Publishing, 1745 Broadway, 20th Floor, New York, NY 10019, USA

Copyright © 2009, 2023
Dorling Kindersley Limited

A Penguin Random House Company

23 24 25 26 10 9 8 7 6 5 4 3 2 1

All rights reserved.

A CIP catalog record is available from the British Library.

A catalog record for this book is available from the Library of Congress.

ISSN 1479-344X

ISBN 978 0 2416 2489 0

Printed and bound in Malaysia

www.dk.com

As a guide to abbreviations in visitor information blocks: **Adm** = *admission charge;* **Av** = *Avenida;* **Btwn** = *between;* **s/n** = *sem número ("no number" in street address).*

MIX
Paper | Supporting responsible forestry
FSC
www.fsc.org
FSC™ C018179

This book was made with Forest Stewardship Council™ certified paper – one small step in DK's commitment to a sustainable future.
For more information go to www.dk.com/our-green-pledge

Phrase Book

In an Emergency

Help!	Socorro!	sookorroo
Stop!	Pare!	pahree
Call a doctor!	Chame um médico!	shamih oong mehjikoo
Call an ambulance!	Chame uma ambulância!	shamih ooma amboolans-ya
Where is the hospital?	Onde é o hospital?	ohnd-yeh oo oshpital
Police!	Polícia!	poolees-ya
Fire!	Fogo!	fohgoo
I've been robbed	Fui assaltado	fwee asaltadoo

Communication Essentials

Yes	Sim	seeng
No	Não	nowng
Hello	Olá	ohla
How are you?	Como vai?	kohmoo vī
Goodbye	Tchau	tshow
See you later	Até logo	ateh logoo
Excuse me	Com licença	kong lisaynsa
I'm sorry	Desculpe	dishkoolp
Thank you	Obrigado (if a man is speaking)/	obrigadoo/
	obrigada (if a woman is speaking)	obrigada
Good morning	Bom dia	bong jeea
Good afternoon	Boa tarde	boh-a tarj
Good night	Boa noite	boh-a noh-itsh
Pleased to meet you	Muito prazer	mweengtoo prazayr
I'm fine	Estou bem/ tudo bem	shtoh bayng/ toodoo bayng
What?	O que?	oo kay
When?	Quando?	kwandoo
How?	Como?	kohmoo
Why?	Por que?	poorkay

Useful Phrases

On the left/right	À esquerda/ direita	a-shkayrda/ jirayta
I don't understand	Não entendo	nowng ayntayndoo
Please speak slowly	Fale devagar por favor	falee jivagar poor favohr
What's your name?	Qual é seu nome?	kwal eh say-oo nohm
My name is…	Meu nome é…	may-oo nohm eh
Go away!	Vá embora!	va aymbora
That's fine	Está bem	shtah bayng
Where is…?	Onde está…?	ohnj shtah

Useful Words

big	grande	granj
small	pequeno	pikaynoo
hot	quente	kayntsh
cold	frio	free-oo
bad	mau	mow
good	bom	bong
open	aberto	abehrtoo
closed	fechado	fishadoo
dangerous	perigoso	pirigohzoo

safe	seguro	sigooroo
first floor	primeiro andar	primayroo andar
ground floor	térreo	tehrryoo
lift	elevador	elevadohr
toilet	banheiro	ban-yayroo
men's	dos homens	dooz ohmaynsh
women's	das mulheres	dash moolyerish
entrance	entrada	ayntrada
exit	saída	sa-eeda
passport	passaporte	pasaportsh

Post Offices and Banks

bank	banco	bankoo
bureau de change	(casa de) câmbio	(kaza jih) kamb-yoo
exchange rate	taxa de câmbio	tasha jih kamb-yoo
post office	correio	koorray-oo
postcard	cartão postal	kartowng pooshtal
postbox	caixa de correio	kisha jih koorray-oo
ATM	caixa automática	kisha owtoomatshika
stamp	selo	sayloo
cash	dinheiro	jeen-yayroo
withdraw money	tirar dinheiro	tshirar jeen-yayroo

Shopping

How much is it?	Quanto é?	kwantweh
I would like…	Eu quero…	ay-oo kehroo
clothes	roupa	rohpa
This one	Esta	ehshta
That one	Essa	ehsa
market	mercado	merkadoo
Do you accept credit cards?	Aceitam cartão de crédito?	asaytowng kartowng jih krehditoo
expensive	caro	karoo

Sightseeing

museum	museu	moozay-oo
art gallery	galeria de arte	galiree-a jih artsh
national park	parque nacional	parkee nas-yoonal
beach	praia	prī-a
river	rio	ree-oo
church	igreja	igray-Ja
cathedral	catedral	katidrow
district	bairro	birroo
garden	jardim	Jardeeng
tourist office	informações turísticas	infoormasoyngsh oreeshtsheekash
guide	guia	gee-a
ticket	bilhete/ ingresso	bil-yaytsh/ ingrehsoo

Transport

bus	ônibus	ohniboosh
boat	barco	barkoo
train	trem	trayng
airport	aeroporto	a-ayroopohrtoo
airplane	avião	av-yowng
flight	vôo	voh-oo
bus stop	ponto de ônibus	pohntoo j- yohniboosh

bus station	**rodoviária**	*roodohvyar-ya*
train station	**estação de trem**	*stasowng jih trayng*
ticket	**passagem**	*pasaJayng*
taxi	**táxi**	*taxee*
subway	**metrô**	*metroh*

Health

I feel bad/ill	**Sinto-me mal/ doente**	*seentoomih mow/dwayntsh*
I need to rest	**Preciso descansar**	*priseezoo jishkansar*
pharmacy	**farmácia**	*farmas-ya*
medicine	**remédio**	*rimehd-yoo*
sanitary towels/ tampons	**absorventes/ tampões**	*absoorvayntsh/ tampoyngsh*
mosquito repellent	**repelente de mosquito**	*ripelayntsh dih mooshkeetoo*
doctor	**médico**	*mehjikoo*
condom	**camisinha**	*kamizeen-ya*

Staying in a Hotel

hotel	**hotel**	*ohteh-oo*
boutique hotel	**pousada**	*pohzada*
guesthouse	**pensão**	*paynsowng*
hostel	**albergue**	*owbehrgee*
Do you have a room?	**Tem um quarto?**	*tayng oong kwartoo*
I have a reservation	**Tenho uma reserva**	*tayn-yoo ooma risehrva*
single/double (room)	**(quarto de) solteiro/casal**	*(kwartoo jih) sooltayroo/ kazow*
towel	**toalha**	*twal-ya*
toilet paper	**papel higiênico**	*papel-oo iJ -yehnikoo*

Eating Out

I want to reserve a table	**Quero reservar uma mesa**	*kehroo rizirvar ooma meyza*
The bill, please	**A conta, por favor**	*a kohnta, poor favohr*
menu	**cardápio/ menu**	*kardap-yoo/ maynoo*
wine list	**lista de vinhos**	*leeshta de veen-yoosh*
glass	**copo**	*kopoo*
bottle	**garrafa**	*garrafa*
restaurant	**restaurante**	*rishtowrantsh*
breakfast	**café da manhã**	*kafeh da man-yang*
lunch	**almoço**	*owmohsoo*
dinner/supper	**jantar**	*Jantar*
(mineral) water	**água (mineral)**	*agwa (minerow)*
vegetarian	**vegetariano**	*vigitar-yanoo*
Is service included?	**O serviço está incluído?**	*oo sirveesoo shtah inklweedoo*

Menu Decoder

açúcar	*asookar*	sugar
alho	*al-yoo*	garlic
arroz	*arrohsh*	rice
azeite	*azaytsh*	olive oil
bebida	*bibeeda*	drink
bem passado	*bayng pasadoo*	well done
bife	*beefee*	steak

café	*kafeh*	coffee
cerveja	*sirvayJa*	beer
chá	*sha*	tea
churrasco	*shoorrashkoo*	barbecue
feijão (preto)	*fayJowng (praytoo)*	(black) beans
frango	*frangoo*	chicken
fruta	*froota*	fruit
lanche	*lanshee*	snack
leite	*laytsh*	milk
pão	*powng*	bread
pimenta	*pimaynta*	pepper
mal passado	*mow pasadoo*	rare
sal	*sow*	salt
vinho	*veen-yoo*	wine
ao ponto	*ow pohntoo*	medium
feijoada	*fayJwada*	bean and meat stew
sorvete	*sohrvaytsh*	ice cream
manteiga	*mantayga*	butter
grelhado	*gril-yadoo*	grilled
batatas fritas	*batatash freetash*	chips
carne	*karnee*	beef
peixe	*payshee*	fish

Time

minute	**minuto**	*minootoo*
hour	**hora**	*ora*
half an hour	**meia hora**	*may-a ora*
Monday	**segunda-feira**	*sigoonda fayra*
Tuesday	**terça-feira**	*tayrsa fayra*
Wednesday	**quarta-feira**	*kwarta fayra*
Thursday	**quinta-feira**	*keenta fayra*
Friday	**sexta-feira**	*sayshta fayra*
Saturday	**sábado**	*sabadoo*
Sunday	**domingo**	*doomeengoo*

Numbers

1	**um/uma**	*oong/ooma*
2	**dois/duas**	*doh-ish/doo-ash*
3	**três**	*traysh*
4	**quatro**	*kwatroo*
5	**cinco**	*seenkoo*
6	**seis**	*saysh*
7	**sete**	*seht*
8	**oito**	*oh-itoo*
9	**nove**	*novee*
10	**dez**	*dehsh*
11	**onze**	*ohnzee*
12	**doze**	*dohzee*
13	**treze**	*trayzee*
14	**catorze**	*katohrzee*
15	**quinze**	*keenzee*
16	**dezesseis**	*dizesaysh*
17	**dezessete**	*dizesehtee*
18	**dezoito**	*dizoh-itoo*
19	**dezenove**	*dizenovee*
20	**vinte**	*veentee*
30	**trinta**	*treenta*
40	**quarenta**	*kwaraynta*
50	**cinqüenta**	*sinkwaynta*
60	**sessenta**	*sesaynta*
70	**setenta**	*setaynta*
80	**oitenta**	*oh-itaynta*
90	**noventa**	*nohvaynta*
100	**cem, cento**	*sayng/sayntoo*

Selected Street Index

1 de Marco, Rua **X2**
7 de Setembro, Rua **W3**
19 de Fevereiro, Rua **Q1**
Afrânio de Melo
Franco, Av **L5**
Aires de Saldanha, Rua
Q5
Alfândega, Rua da **W2**
Almirante Alexandrino,
Rua **V6**
Almirante Barroso, Rua **X3**
Almirante Belford Vieira,
Praça **M5**
Andrè Rebouças, Túnel
F3
Anibal de Mendonca,
Rua **M5**
Antonio Rebouças,
Túnel **F3**
Aprazivel, Rua **U6**
Aqueduto, Rua do **U6**
Araújo Porto Alegre,
Rua **X3**
Arcos, Rua dos **W4**
Aristides Espínola, Rua
K5
Arpoador, Praça do **P6**
Assembléia, Rua **X3**
Ataulfo de Pavia, Av **L5**
Atlântica, Av **Q4**
Augusto Severo, Av **X5**
Barão da Torre, Rua **N5**
Barão de Jaguaripe, Rua
N5
Barão de Petrópolis,
Rua **F3**
Barata Ribeiro, Rua **Q4**
Bartolomeu Mitre,
Av **L5**
Bolívar, Rua **Q4**
Borges de Medeiros, Av
M5
Botafogo, Praia de **H4**
Boticário, Largo do **G3**
Buenos Aires,
Rua de **W2**
Carioca, Rua da **W3**
Carlos Gois, Rua **L5**
Carvalho, Rua de **R3**
Catete, Rua do **W6**
Cinelândia **X4**
Comércio, Travessa de
X2
Conceição, Rua da **V2**
Conde de Bonfim, Rua
D3
Constante Ramos, Rua
Q4
Constituição, Rua da **V3**
Cosme Velho, Rua **G3**
Cupértino Durão, Rua **L5**
Delfim Moreira, Av **L6**
Dias Ferreira, Rua **K5**
Domingos Ferreira, Rua
Q4
Duvivier, Rua **R3**

Eleone de Almeida, Rua
T5
Engenheiro Freyssinet,
Av **F2**
Epitácio Pessoa, Av **N4**
Evaristo da Veiga, Rua
W4
Farme de Amoedo, Rua
N5
Figueireido de
Magalhaes, Rua **Q3**
Fonte da Saudade, Rua
da **N2**
Francisco Bicalho, Av **F1**
Francisco Otaviano, Rua
P6
Frei Caneca, Rua **T4**
Garcia d'Avila, Rua **M5**
General Artigas, Rua **K5**
General Justo, Av **Y3**
General Osório, Praça
P5
General Polidoro, Rua
Q2
General San Martin, Av
L5
General Urquiza, Rua **L5**
General Venâncio
Flores, Rua **L5**
Glória, Ladeira da **X6**
Glória, Rua da **W5**
Gomes Carneiro, Rua **P6**
Gomes Freire, Av **V4**
Gonçalves Dias, Rua **W3**
Gonçalves Ledo, Rua **V3**
Graça Aranha, Av **X3**
Guilhermina Guinle,
Rua **Q1**
Guimarães, Largo dos **V6**
Henrique Dodsworth,
Av **P4**
Henrique Dumont, Av
M5
Henrique Valdares, Av **U4**
Hilário de Gouveia, Rua
Q3
Humaitá, Rua **P2**
Humberto de Campos,
Rua **L5**
Infante dom Henrique,
Av **X5**
Inválidos, Rua dos **V4**
Irmãos, Túnel dois **K5**
Jardel Jercolis, Rua **X4**
Jardim Botânico, Rua **M2**
Joana Angèlica, Rua **N5**
João Lira, Rua **L5**
Joaquim Murtinho, Rua
V5
Joaquim Nabuco, Rua
P6
Joaquim Silva, Rua **W5**
Josè Linhare, Rua **L5**
Kubitschek, Av **X2**
Lagoa-Barra, Estrada **D6**
Lapa, Rua de **W5**

Laranjeiras, Rua das **G3**
Lauro Sodre, Av **R1**
Lavradio, Rua do **V4**
Leme, Ladeira do **R2**
Lineu de Paula
Machado, Av **M3**
Major Vaz, Túnel **Q4**
Maracanã, Av **D3**
Marechal Floriano, Av
U2
Maria Quitèria, Rua **N5**
Marquês de Abrantes,
Rua **H3**
Marquês de São
Vicente, Rua **K4**
Matriz, Rua da **Q1**
Mem de Sá, Av **V4**
Mercado, Rua do **X2**
México, Rua **X4**
Miguel Lemos, Rua **P4**
Monroe, Praça do **X4**
Monte Alegre, Rua **U6**
Nacões Unidas, Av das
H4
Nascimento da Silva,
Rua **M5**
Neves, Largo das **T5**
Niemeyer, Av **K6**
Nilo Peçanha, Av **X3**
Nossa Senhor da Paz,
Praça **N5**
Nossa Senhora de
Copacabana, Av **Q4**
Novo, Túnel **R2**
Oitis, Rua de **K4**
Oriente, Rua do **U5**
Osvaldo Cruz, Av **H3**
Ouvidor, Rua do **W2**
Pacheco Leão, Rua **L3**
Padre Leonel França, Av
K4
Paissandu, Rua **H3**
Paschoal Carlos Magno,
Rua **U6**
Passeio, Rua do **W4**
Passos, Av **V2**
Pasteur, Av **S1**
Paula Freitas, Rua **R3**
Pimentel Duarte, Praça
R1
Pinheiro Machado, Rua
G3
Pio X, Praça **W2**
Pompeu Loureiro, Rua
P4
Portugal, Av **S1**
Pref. Sá Freire Alvim,
Túnel **P5**
Pres Antônio Carlos, Av
X3
Pres Vargas, Av **V2**
Pres Wilson, Av **X4**
Princesa Isabel, Av **S3**
Prof. Alvaro Rodrigues,
Rua **Q1**
Progresso, Rua **U5**

Prudente de Morais,
Rua **N5**
Quitanda, Rua da **X2**
Rainha Elizabeth, Av **P6**
Rainha Guilhermina,
Rua **K5**
Redentor, Rua **M5**
Regente Freijó, Rua **X3**
República do Chile, Av
W3
República do Paraguai,
Av **W4**
República do Peru, Rua
R3
República, Praça da **U3**
Resende, Rua do **V4**
Riachuelo, Rua **T4**
Rio Branco, Av **W2**
Rio Comprido, Túnel **G3**
Rita Ludolf, Rua **K6**
Rodolfo Dantas, Rua **R3**
Rodrigo Otávio, Av **K4**
Rodrigues Alves, Av **F1**
Rosário, Rua do **W2**
Rui Barbosa, Av **H4**
Salvador Sá, Av **G2**
Santa Barbara, Túnel **G3**
Santa Luzia, Rua de **X4**
Santa Teresa, Ladeira de
W5
Santos Dumont, Praça
K4
São Clemente, Rua **Q1**
São João Batista, Rua **Q1**
São José, Rua **X3**
Selarón, Escadaria **W5**
Senado, Rua do **V3**
Senador Dantas, Rua
W4
Senhor dos Passos, Rua
V3
Siqueira Campos, Rua
Q3
Teatro, Rua de **W3**
Teixeira de Freita, Rua
W4
Teixeira de Melo,
Rua **P5**
Tiradentes, Praça **V3**
Tonelero, Rua **Q3**
Uruguaiana, Rua **W3**
Velho, Túnel **Q2**
Vieira Souto, Av **N6**
Vinicius de Moraes, Rua
N5
Visconde de
Albuquerque, Av **K5**
Visconde de Pirajá, Rua
N5
Visconde do Rio
Branco, Rua **U3**
Visconde Inhaúma, Rua
W2
Voluntários da Pátria,
Rua **Q1**
XV, Praça **X2**